STORY WRITING

Also by Edith Ronald Mirrielees

Stanford: The Story of a University
The Writer

Story Writing

by

EDITH RONALD MIRRIELEES

with a Preface by

JOHN STEINBECK

New York · The Viking Press

VIKING COMPASS EDITION
ISSUED IN 1962 BY THE VIKING PRESS, INC.
625 MADISON AVENUE, NEW YORK, N.Y. 10022

FIFTH PRINTING OCTOBER 1970

SBN 670-00111-2

DISTRIBUTED IN CANADA BY
THE MACMILLAN COMPANY OF CANADA LIMITED

THIS EDITION PUBLISHED BY ARRANGEMENT WITH
THE WRITER, INC.

This book is a revised and enlarged version of *The Story Writer,* which appeared in 1939. Thanks for aid in the writing of it, both in the original and in this enlarged form, are due to many people but most of all to my colleagues on the staff of the Bread Loaf Writers' Conference and to the students in my classes at Bread Loaf and at Stanford University.

Excerpts used in the text for which no source is given come either from the writing of students or from my own early stories. For other excerpts, acknowledgment is made in the body of the text and thanks are offered here.

E. R. M.

PRINTED IN THE U.S.A. BY THE MURRAY PRINTING COMPANY

Contents

Preface to the Compass Edition

DEAR EDITH MIRRIELEES:

I am delighted that your volume *Story Writing* is going into a paperback edition. It will reach a far larger audience, and that is a good thing. It may not teach the reader how to write a good short story, but it will surely help him to recognize one when he reads it.

Although it must be a thousand years ago that I sat in your class in story writing at Stanford, I remember the experience very clearly. I was bright-eyed and bushy-brained and prepared to absorb from you the secret formula for writing good short stories, even great short stories. You canceled this illusion very quickly. The only way to write a good short story, you said, is to write a good short story. Only after it is written can it be taken apart to see how it was done. It is a most difficult form, you told us, and the proof lies in how very few great short stories there are in the world.

The basic rule you gave us was simple and heartbreaking. A story to be effective had to convey something from writer to reader, and the power of its offering was the measure of its excellence. Outside of that, you said, there were no rules. A story could be about anything and could use any means and any technique at all—so long as it was effective. As a subhead to this rule, you maintained that it seemed to be necessary for the writer to know what he wanted to say, in short, what he was talking about. As an exercise we were to try reducing the meat of a story to one sentence, for only then could we know it well enough to enlarge it to three or six or ten thousand words.

So there went the magic formula, the secret ingredient. With no more than that you set us on the desolate, lonely path of the writer. And we must have turned in some abysmally bad stories. If I had expected to be discovered in a full bloom of excellence, the grades you gave my efforts quickly disillusioned me. And if I felt unjustly criticized, the judgments of editors for many years afterwards upheld your side, not mine. The low grades on my college stories were echoed in the rejection slips, in the hundreds of rejection slips.

It seemed unfair. I could read a fine story and could even know how it was done, thanks to your training. Why could I not then do it myself? Well, I couldn't, and maybe it's because no two stories dare be alike. Over the years I have written a great many stories and I still don't know how to go about it except to write it and take my chances.

If there is a magic in story writing, and I am convinced that there is, no one has ever been able to reduce it to a recipe that can be passed from one person to another. The formula seems to lie solely in the aching urge of the writer to convey something he feels important to the reader. If the writer has that urge, he may sometimes but by no means always find the way to do it. And if your book, Edith, does nothing more, it will teach many readers to perceive the excellence that makes a good story good or the errors that make a bad story. For a bad story is only an ineffective story.

It is not so very hard to judge a story after it is written, but, after many years, to start a story still scares me to death. I will go so far as to say that the writer who is not scared is happily unaware of the remote and tantalizing majesty of the medium.

I wonder whether you will remember one last piece of advice you gave me. It was during the exuberance of the rich and frantic 'twenties, and I was going out into that world to try to be a writer.

You said, "It's going to take a long time, and you haven't any money. Maybe it would be better if you could go to Europe."

"Why?" I asked.

"Because in Europe poverty is a misfortune, but in America it is shameful. I wonder whether or not you can stand the shame of being poor."

It wasn't too long afterward that the depression came down. Then everyone was poor and it was no shame any more. And so I will never know whether or not I could have stood it. But surely you were right about one thing, Edith. It took a long time—a very long time. And it is still going on, and it has never got easier. You told me it wouldn't.

JOHN STEINBECK

April 1962

PUBLISHERS' NOTE: Edith Mirrielees died on June 3, 1962, at the age of eighty-three. Her revision of the reading lists for this edition of *Story Writing* was received in mid-May.

I

Using This Book

. . . as for the amateur, his difficulty is that his work, once on the page, hardens as cement hardens and can no more be changed. When he has learned to change it, to consider it in this light, to consider it in that, to hold the subject warm in his affections at the same time that his mind appraises the form—when that time comes, he is no longer an amateur.

Suggested Reading

FISCHER, JOHN, and SILVERS, ROBERT B., editors. *Writing in America.* New Brunswick, N.J.: Rutgers University Press.

STEGNER, WALLACE and MARY. Introduction to *Great American Short Stories.* New York: Dell Publishing Company, Laurel Edition.

COWLEY, MALCOLM, editor. *Writers at Work: The* Paris Review *Interviews.* New York: The Viking Press, Compass Books.

MAUGHAM, SOMERSET. *The Summing Up.* New York: Doubleday and Company.

CONRAD, JOSEPH. *A Personal Record.* New York: Doubleday and Company.

MATTHIESSEN, F. O., and MURDOCK, KENNETH B., editors. *The Notebooks of Henry James.* New York: Oxford University Press.

FRANKAU, PAMELA. *Pen to Paper: A Novelist's Notebook.* New York: Doubleday and Company.

Using This Book

I

NEARLY every person who opens this book will do so for a pair of reasons. He will be searching for means of improving all his writing; and he will also be trying to find ways of subduing some one refractory story. The greater part of either struggle has, of course, to go on unaided, but, given sufficient individual effort, certain limited helps may be obtained from the outside. This opening chapter of *Story Writing* purposes to indicate, first, what those helps are—what may and what may not be expected from a book—and, second, how this particular book, which offers no miracles, is meant to be used.

First for the impossibilities: Between the arrival of the idea or feeling which is to grow into a story and the deposit in mind or on paper of its first rough draft, neither a book nor anything else can profitably intervene between the writer and his subject. The best way, even if not necessarily the only way, to write a first draft is to want to write it, to get continually more excited by the thought of it, and finally to sit down and write. How much lies in front of that "finally" differs from writer to writer, but one thing remains true for practically all. Interference in the early stages of a story's growth does harm oftener than good. The title Kipling attached to his record of an upheaval in the subconscious mind, *The Finest Story in the World,* belongs to every story before its incidents are arranged or its first words set down. Anything that interferes with the author's sense of having this time found the finest thing, of being this time about to capture the uncapturable, is injurious to him. That rush of rapture and certitude which comes with the inception of an idea and rarely comes again is among his most valuable writing helps. Those well-meant critical aids—"Wouldn't it be more interesting if you put a woman in the life-boat instead of a man?" "I've thought of something that could happen to him right after he gets home"—may once in a hundred times improve one patchwork story, but they invariably weaken the writer of it. So, too, do the more formal assistances which urge the use of plot outlines and diagrams and other Procrustian stretchings. Writing can never be other than a lonely business. Only by repeated, unaided struggles to shape his yet unwritten material to his own purpose does a beginner grow into a writer. There are a few helps towards general improvement which it is feasible to offer, there are many specific helps in the work of revision, but help in the initial shaping of a story there is none. That is the writer's own affair.

II

It being granted, then, that the thinking out of any one story is the work of the writer and of the writer alone, what help can this book offer in the direction of general improvement? Aided by sufficient intelligent application on the reader's part, it can offer four kinds.

It can increase the amount of meditating about stories.

It can strengthen recognition of the relationship between causes and effect, important in every story.

It can make clear the general application of special happenings.

It can improve use of words, the sole tools a writer has to work with.

To extract any of these helps, however, the reader must make large contributions of his own. Passive reading arrives nowhere.

So far as general improvement is concerned, probably the easiest approach is to read first the chapter, *The Substance of the Story*, reading it through from beginning to end, marking passages likely to be useful to you, blocking off those that do not apply to your kind of writing, putting question marks opposite those you disagree with or feel you have not fully grasped.

This reading is a first step for all readers. Ordinarily, but by no means invariably, the second step is to read one or two of the stories listed at the opening of a chapter, reading not more than one in a day or several days but rereading that one often enough to make yourself familiar with it. You are familiar with it when both the incidents and the thread which holds the incidents together are clear in your mind, when you see why the writer has chosen to open his story at a particular point and to tell it in a particular way. Care has been taken in the selection of stories to set down only those likely to be available in any public library. Though only one source is given for a story, it is usually to be found in a number of places—in the author's collected works, in the magazine of its first appearance, in one or more of the annual short story collections. Not every story set down is for every reader. Rejection of those below or above your present level of appreciation is part of the business of learning.

When one or two· stories are clearly in mind, go back to *Substance* and reread it, changing your markings, jotting in your additions or reservations in the light of what the study of the stories read has taught you. Proceed then to the other chapters in the same slow fashion, reading the chapter, familiarizing yourself with a story or two, rereading the chapter, but broadening the base of your consideration. A story placed under *Time* is as useful for study of substance as though it had been found under the other heading. A story referred to in the chapter on *Substance* might as readily apply to a consideration of time or of character. If you are working as one of a group, your decisions will, of course, be measured against those of the other members. Sometimes the measurement will be to your advantage, but no measure and no outside suggestion can replace steady individual effort at every step in writing.

III

But while you are trying for general improvement, you are also presumably at work on a particular story of your own. In behalf of that story too, it should be remembered that not all of any set of suggestions made in any book is applicable to every writer. The practice you have had, the degree to which you have profited by practice, your native ability, the conditions under which you are working—all of these you need to take account of for yourself. Having taken account, you then modify examples and procedures to fit your own needs.

Let us say that you have, to date, written four stories, each the product of twelve or fourteen hours of labor; that you are now at work on a fifth; and that the four already written have been sent and re-sent to editors, all of them being, in your own eyes, worthy of publication. You are, that is, the very worst variety of amateur, the one who knows not but knows not that he knows not. It is from this depth and by means of your fifth story that you expect a book to assist you.

The first assistance it can give is to cause you to remind yourself that twelve or fourteen hours of effort does not, ordinarily, make a story. It makes only the skeleton of a story, sometimes a mere rib. Expectation of quick results is the bane of amateur writing. There are exceptions certainly, as there are always exceptions, but if your stories are among them, why did none of those earlier four find a place? The time required for learning to write can be shortened, but shortened only in proportion to the genius you happen to possess or to your specially fortunate circumstances. Ordinarily, unless you are prepared to put on your earlier stories as many hours of intelligent effort as go into the carrying and passing of a course in law or medicine, and unless you are ready, too, to admit that one story is to the would-be writer only what one course is to the prospective doctor or lawyer, then probably you would be wise to tear up that fifth story and turn what persistence you have in another direction. If, however, you do have the persistence for keeping on, you sit down with the completed draft of your story in front of you—that draft which, without outside warning, you would have been shipping off to some magazine. It is already as nearly perfect as you know how to make it. If it is to be better, it has to be through your learning to see and remedy its imperfections.

Probably you have already been asking yourself along the way what your story is about. Unless you have, there is no use in asking now. If you have thought a story through without knowing what idea holds its parts together, you will discover, if at all, only by way of the rearranging and chipping and rubbing which go to make up revision. Or it may be you are one of the writers who need never consciously consider the foundation ideas of their stories. At any rate, begin with questions more limited.

Reread your opening pages with your attention fixed on one matter only—say, the placing of your incidents in time. Do they show the time at which the telling begins? Why does it begin at that point? What have the paragraphs preceding the first time break contributed to the story? When you have answered these questions to your satisfaction or partial satisfaction, read slowly through the whole story, marking, in mind or margin, the transitions by which it moves from one point in time to another, noting omissions of any considerable blocks of time and accounting to yourself both for the omissions and for the way in which you have made readers aware of them. That done, lay the story aside for a day or two. Within these days, read the chapter on *Time,* marking, blocking and questioning as in *Substance*. Select a story from the list given at the beginning of the section and read it, bringing the passages just marked to bear on it. Does it uphold them? Or can you—remember we are making you the worst of amateurs—see simply no connection at all? If this is true, choose another story and apply to it one, and only one, of the simpler suggestions in the text, perhaps "—the time of a happening in the story and the intervals between happening and happening must be kept clear." With this new story keep your mind fixed only on time changes. After you have gone carefully over some other writer's story, turn back to your own and consider it with the sentence quoted above and that sentence only in mind, blocking in, however awkwardly, the changes required to keep time clear. This being done, try another passage from the text against a story—say, the passage dealing with general and inciting causes. Do not try it against your own story until you feel you have been successful with one not your own.

In any story of your own, there will be some things about which you are sure from the beginning. You are sure, for example, that a long time—a year, ten years—must intervene between beginning and end; you are sure the story must be told from a given point of observation. Otherwise it will not be yours, will not be what you have set out to write. These are certainties not to be tampered with. No matter what advice, written or spoken, points in another direction, your story has to stay yours. It should change only as you feel it ought to change. Even though your feeling is wrong, it is better for your ultimate success to be wrong than to be spineless. But in matters where you do not have a fixed conviction, bring story against chapter in the fashion just suggested, allowing yourself frequent opportunity for trying your impressions on stories not your own. When story number five has come again to what seems to you perfection, or when your mind has become so confused about it that you can no longer make decisions, put five away to cool, working on four or six until five is ready for further improvement.

All this labor, this analysis of other people's stories and of your own, this revising and putting away to cool, means staying a long time with one story. Most stories that are to be stories need to be stayed with a long time. Especially most beginners' stories do. Whether that staying is to be done before the first word comes to paper or whether it is to be done after the rough draft is set down is a matter of individual habit, but somewhere time has to be spent. Flitter-mindedness—a new idea every week and interest in the old one dead and gone—is one of the handicaps that keep a would-be writer would-be and no more to the end of his writing days.

"But" asks that worst of amateurs who momentarily is you, "won't working with other people's stories make me imitative, hurt my originality?" The answer to that familiar question is a flat no. In the long run, nobody writes like anybody but himself—a self made up, as all selves are, of scraps pieced together from everywhere. Smothering yourself under a deluge of stories is as bad as any other form of smothering, but reading, pondering on, above all rereading, those stories to which you feel a kinship is an exercise from which only good can come. There exist writers who are not constant and sedulous readers, but their number is not large.

Suggested Reading

O'CONNOR, FLANNERY. "The Displaced Person," in *A Good Man is Hard to Find, and Other Stories*. New York: Harcourt, Brace and World.

GOLD, HERBERT. "The Panic Button," in *Love and Like*. New York: The Dial Press.

CONRAD, JOSEPH. "The Shadow Line," in *The Shadow Line*. New York: Doubleday and Company.

MCKINLEY, GEORGIA. "The Fragile Heaven." *Virginia Quarterly Review*, Winter 1962.

USTINOV, PETER. "Add a Dash of Pity," in *Add a Dash of Pity*. Boston: Atlantic–Little, Brown and Company.

LENNON, PETER. "Adult Company." *The New Yorker*, May 12, 1962.

GREENE, GRAHAM. "The Basement Room," in *Twenty-One Stories*. New York: The Viking Press.

STEELE, WILBUR DANIEL. "The Man Who Saw Through Heaven," in *The Best Stories of Wilbur Daniel Steele*. New York: Doubleday and Company.

II

The Substance of the Story

To understand social reality, one must be inside it, participate in its movements and its struggles.

—IGNAZIO SILONE, *Bread and Wine*

The Substance of the Story

I

"There is a limit to the profitable elaboration of the obvious."

THE originator of the above quotation is unknown, but internal evidence points towards his having been the reader for some large-size, fiction-publishing weekly.

In one sense it is true, as asserted in nearly every discussion of fiction writing, that there is no such thing as stale material, that any human situation lends itself to fictive treatment. Nonetheless, stories fail for staleness, for lack of substance, for elaboration of the obvious, even oftener than from the writer's not knowing how to bring out what he intends to say. One of the questions a beginner at writing is called upon to put to himself when his first draft is finished, and often even earlier than that, is "What is my story about?" If he arrives at the answer, "It is about Herbert's marrying Sylvia," then the question should be put again and with a stronger emphasis, "But what is it *about?*" A story is almost never only about the marriage of Herbert to Sylvia any more than it is only about a shipwreck or a battle or a death or the finding of a gold mine. Now and then a writer writes a really good story without himself realizing, at any stage in the writing, what that story is, but such an adventure is rare. In the thinking out of most stories, the thing the story is about, as apart from merely what happens in it, is of the utmost importance.

For a story is not the sum of its happenings.

That statement deserves the dignity of a paragraph to itself. With the fewest exceptions a story is never merely a problem in addition, occurrence added to occurrence till the telling is done. To see why it is not, it is necessary only to look at daily living, the source material for all fiction.

For any being living it, life is more than the march of successive happenings. A bookkeeper goes to his office, bends over his books, lunches at a neighboring drug store, goes home to listen to his radio, to fret at his wife. Does this make up life for him? His life is no such flat and open page. What does make it up is the many-colored thread of feeling which runs through the happenings and gives cohesion to them. Dread of poverty, anxiety about his family's future, an artist's pleasure in his own exactness, a dream of advancement to come, an odd-hours' hobby, a dogged loyalty—any or all of these may be components of the thread. And each important component is both a part of the bookkeeper's inner life and also some small fraction of the inner life of any reader who can comprehend or be interested in him. The incidents of the two lives may have no point in common, but except superficially it is not the incidents for which the reader reads. It is for the man concerned in them. Incident piled on incident no more makes life than brick piled on brick makes a house. Neither does incident piled on incident make a story. Something beyond the incidents is essential to turn a set of happenings into fiction.

One chief importance of grasping the difference between piled happenings and stories is that, really grasped, the understanding of that difference regulates a beginner's writing habits. For since a story is other than the sum of its incidents, the reiterated truths about the uses of practice are half-truths only. Practice is indeed essential to writing, as essential as to violin playing. But practice alone accomplishes nothing. It may go on day in and day out, has gone on so through years, with a grinding, unflagging, heartbreaking persistence, and yet has produced no marked improvement in output. A writer's belief that persistence is all and is bound to be rewarded has no more foundation than that other belief, common to those who do not write, that authorship arrives by unaided inspiration. For fiction, if it is to be readable, comes not out of one thing but out of two—first, out of having something to say; and second, out of an unending diligence in trying to say it. Most of the chapters in this book deal with ways of saying it. This one deals with the even more important matter of having something to say.

To have that something, it is by no means necessary to have undergone bizarre experiences. Not many people have had unusual adventures; all people, without exception, have had adventures enough to provide for lifetimes of story writing. Everybody has been a child, has grown up, fallen in love, fallen out of love. Everybody has experienced self-pity, self-approval, the anguish of loss by death, the slower anguish of loss by disillusionment. These are the things which make stories. These are the things which make them whether the stories are laid in Turkestan or New Jersey. It is not lack of experience which handicaps any writer. What it is, is the purblindness that prevents his seeing, or his seeing into, the experiences he has had.

If a beginner is enough in earnest really to have studied

the form he is attempting to use, he will already have put sufficient thought on some published stories to have discovered what those stories are about and how the writer made him aware of what they are about. He will have recognized that the happenings are, individually, like beads, serving their purpose only because a cord unites them. This cord is the central idea, the underlying idea, of the whole story.

A storyteller, then, is always doing two things and doing them simultaneously. He is picturing certain portions of individual lives, and at the same time he is showing some larger, some more general matter, of which those lives are the example. What the pieces of life illustrate may be a maxim or the denial of a maxim; it may be the effect of environment, race, economic placing; it may be the progress of an inevitable destiny. Whatever it is, idea and incident march together. The individual figures move in the foreground of the story; accompanying them, as a man is accompanied by his shadow, appears that which they exemplify.

Which is the more important, action or idea, man or shadow, depends upon where the writer places his emphasis. In allegory, the shadow is important. In narratives of adventure, the importance of the general idea is frequently only a little greater than that of an actual shadow at midnight. It is safe to say, though, that in any story which sticks in the mind the shadow has a visible place. Presentation and representation go on together.

An easily identified example of this double progress is found in Joseph Conrad's *The Shadow Line*. The young captain's obtaining of his command; his discovery of the lack of quinine; his struggle, grotesque and dreadful, against his first mate's obsession—these are happenings of absorbing interest. But at no time are readers unaware that what holds the happenings in place and gives them meaning is their effect on the captain's soul. His passage is externally from port to port. His more important passage is across that line which cuts off youth from maturity.

Seventy Thousand Assyrians, by William Saroyan, emphasizes as definitely the dominance of idea over incident. Here the incidents themselves are related only in time. The teller chances to see one person, chances to see another, carries on certain conversations, thinks certain thoughts. What gives direction to his otherwise aimless progress is the fierce heat of a central idea. As in the allegory, the shadow is far more important than the figures casting it.

A writer finds himself possessed of an idea which worries in his brain until he arrives at appropriate actions and persons to express it; or his imagination is seized by certain people or happenings over which he mulls till their general importances grow partly clear to him. One thing or the other having happened, his story comes into being.

II

A story, then, must not only tell something; it must also be about something. In your individual story Herbert, let us say, is to be shown falling in love with Sylvia and finally winning her. Well, Herberts have fallen in love with Sylvias, have won them or lost them, since time began. Why should a reader be interested this time?

The reasons why he should be—why, decade after decade, he continues to be—have more to do with what Herbert represents, with the kind of shadow he casts, than with what he actually presents.

One of the most frequent of presentations is that of Herbert struggling against obstacles seemingly insuperable. From the time of David and Goliath, and probably long before, the story of the weak conquering the strong, of the strong destroyed by a pebble, has been assured of readers' interest. It has been because the reader's habit in reading is similar to his habit in daily experience. Passing a man on the sidewalk, one of a thousand on his way home from work, he barely sees him or sees him not at all. Passing the same man struggling to street level from a suddenly opened crevice, clinging to a window ledge high above the street, he not only sees him, he stops to stare and cannot go on till the crisis has resolved itself—man proved stronger than obstacle, obstacle stronger than man. Those stories in which Herbert is a bank clerk and Sylvia the bank president's daughter, Herbert a divinity student and Sylvia a night-club singer, draw their essential interest not from Herbert's love, which is more or less taken for granted, but from the question of whether, through the impulse of that love, he can get free of what impedes him. Can he climb out of his pit? Can he get safely down from his high ledge? What kind of hindrances he is to meet, how many, how obvious, depends upon the kind of writer you are—upon your view of life. But if your story is to hold a reader's interest, there has to be in it an implied generalization as well as a special case. The reader has to see in Herbert's success or failure an exemplification of some part of his own philosophy or to find in Herbert some vague identification with himself or his neighbor. Otherwise Herbert is merely dull to read of.

Apart from the interest produced by struggle against obstacles, the next most usual source of interest is surprise. Reduced to essentials, the qualities which make up a surprise story are found, all of them, in the familiar anecdote of the Western Union messenger boy delivering his first death message. The boy—inexperienced, impressionable, afraid— lingers in front of the apartment house, pushes the bell reluctantly, hears with dread the approaching footsteps. The girl who comes to the door opens the envelope, scans the sheet, shouts up the stairs, "Ma, Uncle Henry's dead." From above comes the shouted answer, "Well, it's about time." What the anecdote does is what the surprise story always has to do; it takes a situation expected to produce one result and shows it producing another.

Thus far, analysis is easy. Unless it goes farther, it is also worthless. Every year there are written probably a ton of would-be surprise stories which produce a reversal of expectation and nothing else. Their writers have failed to take into account that, if the reversal is to accomplish its end, close on the heels of surprise must come a recognition of the truth of what is shown. In *Rachel Mourning for Her Children,* by Frances Newman, the mother of an only child sits quiet beside her son-in-law through her daughter's funeral service, bursts into unrestrained weeping only at its end. Throughout the service, she has reviewed her life— a passive child under domineering parents, a passive wife under a domineering husband, a passive widow established in the home of a domineering daughter. Never—and she is moving towards sixty—never till now has she foreseen the opportunity to select her own clothes, dispose of her own time, pour tea for her own friends from the teapot of her choice. The close of the service breaks in on her reverie; she rises and, as she does so, observes from across the aisle a widow's acquisitive eye turned full upon the grief-drenched widower.

Both reversals of expectation—her unexpected meditations, her unexpected tears—take the reader by surprise, but both, too, instantly convince him.

Stories based on surprise, that is, are stories which note exceptions. Experience shows that exceptions are as true as rules. A death brings sorrow—but not always. A wedding is a scene of joy—but again, not always. A mother loves her child—but sometimes too she hates it. Let it be repeated —in view of beginners' habits, it cannot be repeated too often—that surprise alone has no fictional value. The only kind capable of supporting a story is the kind which, on second thought, ceases to be surprise at all.

Both in *Rachel Mourning for Her Children* and in Jacobs' *A Question of Habit,* referred to in another chapter, surprise is bound up with situation. It is sometimes dependent on wording only. A story appearing in one of the later issues of *Hound and Horn* records, with a luxuriance of detail, the griefs and dangers of a woman captured by Indians. The story of her capture, her enslavement, her final escape, leaves out no particle of horror. A bare rifle-shot's length ahead of her pursuers, she reaches the safety of a blockhouse. As she falls inside the gate, her emotions find outlet in a closing sentence, "I'm sure glad to get shut of them Indians." The contrast between extremity of peril and commonplaceness of speech is effective only because, simultaneously with the shock of that inadequacy, comes the reader's recognition that just so she would have spoken. The rhetoric to match her torments lies in the reader's mind, not hers.

Assertion of a philosophic principle, assertion or denial of a maxim lies at the base of many stories. Bret Harte's *The Luck of Roaring Camp,* Edward Everett Hale's *The Man Without a Country,* the more recent *Address Unknown,* by Kressmann Taylor, are items on a list any reader can prolong at will. And any careful reader, considering these and other stories, finds three things true of the underlying ideas of all of them. Briefly put, the three are these:

The underlying idea of a story is never original with the writer of it.

An underlying idea need not be, and seldom is, universally true.

A story may embody more than one underlying idea.

The first of these three—that an underlying idea is never original—is all but self-evident. Particular incidents may be the writer's own invention or his own rearrangement. Underlying ideas are always the crystallizations of wide-spread human experience. If it were otherwise—if a writer could, as he cannot, invent an underlying idea—his story would be unintelligible. Conversely, the more widely accepted the underlying idea he embodies, the wider his audience is likely to be. This is not because the widely accepted is necessarily the truer. "Love's not Time's fool" may be no truer to any given situation, or even truer in any greater number of situations, than its obverse; it only, in most decades, is more heart-warming, and therefore more readily acceptable, to numbers of readers.

Second, an underlying idea need not be universally true. "A little child shall lead them" serves for foundation for *The Luck of Roaring Camp* and hundreds of other stories because much experience points that way, though there are also experiences sharply contradictory. In the terms of readers' emotions, "God's in His Heaven: all's right with the world" is "true" today; "The God who shapes the tortured flesh and damns the babe unborn" equally "true" tomorrow. The two ideas cannot reside in the same story nor be received in the mind at the same moment, but each can have its turn there. Notoriously, every maxim has its counter-maxim. "Soft words butter no parsnips.". . . "A soft answer turneth away wrath." "Look before you leap.". . . "Slow choosers are losers." Either one of either pair is upheld by enough experiences to give it standing. *Young Ames,* Walter D. Edmonds' story of the youth who risks humiliation and loss of job for one more glimpse of his employer's niece, is based on a whole handful of accepted maxims. In James Stephens' *Three Lovers Who Lost,* the story of the second lover reverses those same maxims. Not only is each story acceptable to some readers, but both may be acceptable to the same reader, who at one moment enjoys the exemplified rule, at another the exemplified exception.

Third, as several of the stories already named point out, a story is not limited to one underlying idea. One main idea it usually has, but one may underlie another like skins in an onion, so long as no one contradicts any of the rest.

For getting these three qualities of the underlying idea firmly in mind, a would-be writer can do worse than to re-consider Bret Harte's *The Outcasts of Poker Flat,* where what the story rests on is so obviously—not to say, so blatantly—expressed that it cannot readily be overlooked. The figures in the story are a gambler, a sluicebox robber, two prostitutes, and two young innocents eloping to be married who fall in with the quartet by chance. The story illuminates first that "so much good in the worst of us" which has provided the motive for even more fiction than has its accompanying "so much bad in the best of us." It points out also that appearances are deceitful, and, in showing them to be so, that youthful innocence is contagious to all around it, which last is, again, "A little child shall lead them." None of the ideas is original; all are truths but only partial truths; one fits neatly to the rest. And because each is supported by a good deal of experience and is comfortably at home therefore in a multitude of minds, they account probably even more than the story's exotic setting for its immediate popularity and for its having stayed alive through three quarters of a century.

Hawthorne's *David Swan*, the story of a youth approached while asleep and left behind still asleep, by love, by fortune, and by death, is an example of trivial incident given importance by the acceptability of its idea. His even better known *The Ambitious Guest* rests on an idea at home at one time or another in every mature human mind.

The stories quoted so far are serious ones. Emphasis on underlying idea does not necessarily predicate seriousness. "One born every minute," "The leopard cannot change his spots"—these have oftener than not had humorous presentations, and each has had very many. In Edith Wharton's *The Mission of Jane*, the well worn "A little child shall lead them" produces in readers more mirth, though of an acrid flavor, than it produces pity. Katharine Brush's *Night Club*, however bitter, is laugh-producing too.

It has been already said that underlying ideas are group products of long growth. Two other things should be added. The first of these is that only to a very limited extent does a writer select what ideas he will deal with. What he himself is, what rock foundation his beliefs about existence rest on, tends to show in his writing whether he wills it or not. Hence, the hosts of the unsuccessful who, against their own convictions, and in the hope of publishing, struggle with happy endings or their opposites according to which way the tide is flowing. O. Henry's "Write what you like; there is no other rule," is, like other positives, subject to a certain discount, but the discount is very small indeed as concerns the ideas in a story which lie below its incidents.

The second of the two truths, which superficially seems to contradict the first, is that, long-lasting as ideas are, some of them do eventually become outworn. Almost any story by Hannah More—preferably *The Shepherd of Salisbury Plain* or *'Tis All for the Best*; many of Maria Edgeworth's; three-fourths of those appearing in the nineteenth century New England annuals suffer with present readers not because of their old-fashioned deliberateness of telling but because the theses governing them are no longer acceptable. It is worth a would-be writer's while to turn back to one or two of these examples and to contrast them with the equally elderly *Legend of Sleepy Hollow*, kept perennially acceptable by its underlying ideas quite as much as by felicity of wording.

Obstacles past which the hero struggles; surprise which shows an end to action unforeseen but logical; elucidation of individual character with yet enough of the general to be in part indentified with reader or reader's neighbor; happenings fitted together to deny or support a maxim or to make clear an unsaid prophecy—any of these give a story connection and point. Some of them you are fairly sure to discover as you turn over in mind the memorable stories you have read.

When you return to your own unsatisfying one, your first necessity is to make clear to yourself what that particular story is meant to tell. Some things it will tell without co-operation on your part—something of your personal philosophy, the clarity or muddle of your thinking, the accuracy or inaccuracy of your observation. These unavoidables, however, are not your concern. What is your concern is why a piece of writing into which you have put effort is unacceptable even in the eyes of its maker. Have you a story? Or have you only a series of details, collated but not connected? If there is a story, is it ineffective because of the kind of ideas which hold the incidents together? Do outworn generalizations, incompatible ones, lie beneath the surface of the action? What is the story *about?*

III

The question asked in Section II is asked of stories already formed in mind or already on paper. Earlier still, as he watches what goes on around him, two other questions tease at the brain of any would-be writer. One of these is,

"What will happen?" The other is, "What would happen if
—?" According to the kind of writer you are, the first or
the second fascinates you.

"What will happen?" looks, of course, to deduction from
observable circumstances. "What would happen if—?" looks
to a readjustment of those circumstances through the intru-
sion of some deciding condition created by the writer. Frances Frost's "Piano Prelude" is a story answering the first
question; Elmer Davis's "Bride of Quietness," one answering the second.

In "Piano Prelude" readers see, through the eyes of a
seven-year-old child, a family of three drifting towards
wretchedness and towards the child's moral ruin because of
the mother's irritable and suspicious temper. The mother's
outbursts, the child's answering flare-ups of bewildered anger, the timid conciliations of the father—all of these are
within every reader's experience, whether at first hand or
vicariously. The writer isolates happenings which concern
the child, records the child's response to them; she adds no
alleviations, injects nothing unexpected. Since the situation
and the relations of the three members of the family are
thoroughly comprehensible, what is to come—what must
come—is implicit in what is presented. The scene once set,
the story moves on implacably. Not only the hours covered
by it, but the years lying beyond stand out clear and unchangeable in the reader's mind.

In "Bride of Quietness" a man returns to a class reunion
at the college from which he has been graduated years earlier. It is his first return. To his consternation, he discovers
the magnificent boys, the potential world-changers of his
undergraduate recollection, have grown thin of hair and

thick at waistline, solidified in opinions as in body. The dream-challenging girls are comfortably dowdy or stridently oversmart. So far, the second story is as much the presentation of a familiar situation, even if an exaggerated one, as is the first. But it is not "What will happen?" which interests its writer, it is "What would happen if—?" If, for instance, among this mob of disheartening contemporaries, there were to appear one glorious being, the class beauty, looking exactly, looking indistinguishably, except for bobbed hair and shortened skirts, as she had looked that last night in senior week—what then would happen?

Recording what will happen is a matter of observation, of analysis, of identification of writer with subject. Recording what would happen *if*, is the exercise of a mind awake to incongruities. One strong tie, however, unites the two kinds of stories. Characters, conditions, and exceptions being established, a writer of either kind must stay within the limits he has set. In order to stay within them, he must do three things—keep his story to what its opening has promised; keep his people fundamentally, even if not externally, consistent; and hold his individual incidents within the bounds of that especial plausibility the story establishes. Henry James, Theodore Dreiser, Ruth Suckow, Frances Frost are writers who devote themselves to stories showing what will happen. Any short story written by them, followed to its end, leaves room for no conclusion but the one set down. Stella Benson, H. G. Wells, John Collier, though sometimes "What will happen?" absorbs them, are still more likely to be absorbed by "What would happen *if*—".

III

Repetition

"I have said it once,
I have said it twice,
When I say it three times—"
                    Lewis Carroll
                        The Hunting of the Snark.

Suggested Reading

OLSEN, TILLIE. "I Stand Here Ironing," in *Tell Me a Riddle.* Philadelphia and New York: J. B. Lippincott Company.

WELTY, EUDORA. "Why I Live at the P.O.," in *A Curtain of Green and Other Stories.* New York: Harcourt, Brace and World.

WHITE, ROBIN. "The New Blanket," in *Foreign Soil: Tales of South India.* New York: Atheneum.

POE, EDGAR ALLAN. "The Pit and the Pendulum," in many story collections.

DAHL, ROALD. "Taste," in *Someone Like You.* New York: Alfred A. Knopf.

O'CONNOR, FRANK. "The Idealist," in *Stories by Frank O' Connor.* New York: Alfred A. Knopf, Vintage Books.

CONRAD, JOSEPH. "Youth," in *Youth.* New York: Doubleday and Company.

Repetition

Once upon a time there lived a king who was very great but also very greedy. Every year he took the corn his subjects raised, and stored it away in a great granary to sell when prices were high . . . But though the doors were sealed and the windows were sealed and nobody could get in, there was one thing the builder had forgotten. Up in the eaves was a tiny hole where the bricks had not quite fitted together, and one day a swarm of locusts flew past, and one of the locusts found the tiny hole and flew in. When he came out, he carried off a grain of corn, and another locust came and carried off another grain of corn, and another locust came and carried off another grain of corn, and another locust came—

THERE is no reason why the story should not go on indefinitely. There is plenty of corn, there are plenty of locusts. The only shortage is in the patience of the reader. But though the reader who is only a reader will abandon the locust story early, the reader who is also a writer will read far enough to find in it a definite usefulness. Like all parodies, it gets its effect from exaggeration, but what it exaggerates is an important principle—in this instance, the essential principle that repetition is a means, and a chief means, for shaping raw material into story.

No matter what the kind of story, the writer of it must tap repeatedly on the same spot—"and another locust came and carried off another grain of corn, and another locust came. . . ." He must do also, though, one other thing which the teller of the locust story neglects. Tapping on one spot, he yet must vary the sound of every tap. The reconciling of these two seemingly contradictory requirements is basic to all story making. What is to impress a reader must be repeated and re-repeated, ground into his mind by repetition. And yet each repetition, though it must be like the rest in kernel, must differ in outer shell.

This necessity of combining difference and likeness—of saying a thing over and over and yet so saying it that the reader accepts it as new—is a root difficulty of all writing. Especially it is the difficulty of the short story, where space for saying is small. "Line upon line and precept upon precept" is applied oftenest to the teaching of morals. It is equally efficient in the practice of writing. Anybody can think of the inciting incident for a story; the world is full of them. Or if he cannot, all he need do is pick up a volume of familiar quotations or unfold a daily paper. Almost anybody, having been seized by the desire to write a particular story, can find a beginning, even if not a good one, and frequently an end. Where the story sags is in the middle.

This sag is discoverable by any writer merely by reading over the first drafts of his own earlier work. Either what he is telling is reduced to anecdotal proportions, or the central pages wander off from what he has intended them to say. Or if these misfortunes are avoided, the central pages deaden interest by their monotony. How much repetition a story calls for, how obvious it should be, depends partly on the story itself, partly on the audience for which it is intended. In children's stories, undisguised repetition is one of the accepted charms. Because it is, repetition is sometimes thought of as belonging there only. Actually, when a writer tries to express a complicated idea for an audience adult and sophisticated, what he decreases is not the number of repetitions by which he drives home his point but only the openness with which they are allowed to force themselves on attention.

Let us look first at the child's story.

And the Little Wee Bear said in his little wee voice, "Somebody's been sleeping in my bed!"
And the Middle-sized Bear said in his middle-sized voice, "Somebody's been sleeping in my bed too!"
And the Great Big Bear said in his great big voice, "Somebody's been sleeping in my bed! AND HERE SHE IS!"

Without a little bear and a middle-sized bear preceding the big one, making the same discovery, saying the same words, that climactic "And here she is!" would lose nine-tenths of its effect. It is effective not because it is unforeseen, but for precisely the opposite reason. It has been so long foreseen that the reader's mind has had time to move forward with the storyteller's. The discovery of Goldilocks affects him in proportion to the length and intensity of his expectation of that discovery, not in proportion to his astonishment.

And what is true in *The Three Bears* is also true elsewhere. The actually unexpected is rarely effective. Mary Lamb, springing up suddenly from the placid family supper table to stab her mother, is possible in life. In fiction, she is not—not unless, tap after tap, unobtrusively, unfailingly, "There is danger, there is danger" has been hammered home into the reader's consciousness. Without that hammering home, what should be horrifying is ludicrous instead.

Stories devoted to the elucidation of one particular emotion or characteristic make, of course, the easiest studies of how repetition may be used. Poe's *Tales of Horror*, ground down as these usually are to their very essentials, can scarcely be avoided as examples. *William Wilson, The Pit and the Pendulum, The Black Cat, The Premature Burial*—each asks only that the reader shall recognize the presence and the growth of a certain kind of fear. Character is of no account; incidents are solely to embody the evidence by which fear is established. Poe, that is, set himself the hardest of all tasks, the securing of variety in incidents with most of the means of attaining variety already excluded.

The Pit and the Pendulum is perhaps the most useful for detailed consideration. What readers of the story are asked to believe in is the presence of impending death, seemingly inescapable and in hideous form. They have no acquaintance with the hero's personality, none but the slightest intimation concerning his past. What is sought is not sympathy or repulsion towards an individual, only certitude on the reader's part of the actuality of peril. The reader is to be convinced of that peril, to shudder at it, to feel relief when it is avoided. To reach these ends, the writer must keep peril steadily in the foreground and yet must repeatedly alter its aspect.

Poe accomplishes this end by presenting first a series of differing dangers. The earliest is the danger of falling into an unseen opening in the dungeon floor; the second, the descent of death in the form of a slowly moving blade beneath which the victim is fastened; the third, death through the hot walls' pressing the victim into the now seen, though not described, pit.

Each episode offers death, the ultimate of all dangers. Each offers it in a peculiarly dreadful form. Each dreadful form differs from its predecessors. Alteration of kind of

danger, however, standing alone, does not constitute a sufficient variety. Beyond this, each prospective death appeals
to a new nightmare terror, one which has figured in the
dreams of almost every reader—the terror of falling, the terror of being caught immovable in the track of danger, the
terror of being burned. Each danger in turn is avoided by
means not only in themselves different but springing from
a different source. The first time, the hero trips on the torn
hem of his robe and falls forward over the edge of the unseen pit, thus discovering it before he is precipitated into
it—escape by sheer accident. The second time, he rubs the
fats from his dishes of food over the leather thongs which
bind him and so persuades the rats swarming in his dungeon to gnaw him free—escape through his own ingenuity.
The third time, "The fiery walls rushed back. An out-
stretched arm caught my own as I fell, fainting, into the
abyss. . . . The Inquisition was in the hands of its enemies"
—escape through outside aid.

Each set of shifts, taken by itself, is unimportant, but
by means of all of them, the reader's attention is not dis-
tracted by over-emphasis on the hero's ingenuity nor yet by
over-consciousness of luck working in his favor, and still is
kept constantly fixed on his danger. The reader believes in
that danger because it is vividly presented again and again.
He does not weary of it because each presentation differs
not only in one particular but in a series of them from every
other.

To show a thing over and over, to give to each showing
a different color—these are the elementary requirements for
all repetition. Even in *The Three Bears*, where the first is
paramount, the second requirement has still to be satisfied.

Chair gives place to bowl and bowl to bed before the final discovery.

An example more complicated than *The Pit and the Pendulum* is Susan Glaspell's *A Jury of Her Peers*. Told in the third person with entrance into the mind of only one of the two women concerned, the story covers the hour in which the two wait in the house of a neighbor who has been removed the day before to the county jail on the charge of having murdered her husband. While they wait, the county attorney and the women's husbands, one of them the sheriff, search the premises for evidence which shall show a motive for the killing. Left in the kitchen while the men examine elsewhere, the women find that evidence and enter into a mute compact to conceal it. The story this time has not one set of repetitions but three, each supporting the other two. There are the repetitions which convince the waiting women, themselves wives, that the wife did do the killing; there are those which justify her in their eyes; and there are those which bind them together, as women, in defense of a woman. The last of the three sets is brief enough to allow for partial quotation.

The county attorney . . . paused and looked around the kitchen.

"You're convinced there was nothing important here?" he asked the sheriff. "Nothing that would point to any motive?"

The sheriff too looked all around as if to reconvince himself.

"Nothing here but kitchen things," he said, with a little laugh for the insignificance of kitchen things.

Before the men go upstairs to the room where the killing took place, they discover that the preserved fruit in the

cupboard has frozen and burst. The sheriff's wife mentions
that the prisoner was worrying for fear it would.

Mrs. Peters' husband broke into a laugh. "Well, can you beat
the women! Held for murder, and worrying about her preserves!" . . .
"Oh, well," said Mrs. Hale's husband with good-natured supe-
riority, "women are used to worrying over trifles."

As the three men start up the stairs, the county attorney
suggests that perhaps Mrs. Hale or Mrs. Peters may come
across a clue.

Mr. Hale rubbed his face in the fashion of a showman getting
ready for a pleasantry.
"But would the women know a clue if they did come on it?"
he asked.

Nothing is found upstairs. The searchers return to discover the two women looking at the prisoner's partly finished
quilt.

Just as the stair door opened, Mrs. Hale was saying, "Do you
suppose she was going to quilt it or just knot it?"
The sheriff threw up his hands.
"They wonder whether she was going to quilt it or just knot it!"
There was a laugh for the ways of women . . .

In the meantime the women have been finding evidence
in abundance—raggedly uneven sewing on one block, and
only one, of the partly pieced quilt; a dishcloth left lying
on the half-washed table; the door of a birdcage swing-
ing on a broken hinge. Finally, in a box beneath the quilt

squares, they come on final proof—a dead bird, its head dangling from a wrung neck. At sight of the dead bird, they see the reason for the murder, the necessity upon the wife to commit it in exactly the way she did, her utter justification.

"We all go through the same things—it's all just a different kind of the same thing. If it weren't—why do you and I understand? Why do we know—what we know this minute?"

They rip out the betraying stitches, conceal the dead bird in Mrs. Hale's pocket. The men return with nothing to show for their search.

"Well, Henry," said the county attorney facetiously, "at least we found out one thing. She was not going to quilt it. She was going to—what do you call it, ladies?"

Mrs. Hale's hand was against the pocket of her coat.

"We call it—knot it, Mr. Henderson." *

As *A Jury of Her Peers* makes plain, the need for repetition is not confined to the main idea of a story or to its immediately supporting ideas. Every important trait or mannerism, every significance of landscape, requires to be impressed on the mind by repeated presentation. In *An Outpost of Progress,* by Joseph Conrad, the wretched white in charge of the trading post hangs himself at last from the arm of the tall cross which marks his predecessor's grave. Casually, ironically, the presence of that cross, its size, its strength,

* "A Jury of Her Peers," by Susan Glaspell, was first published in *Every Week.*

its fitness as an instrument of execution, has been brought home to the reader in the earlier pages. Each time it has been done in a paragraph so weighted with other importances that the mention was subsidiary and illustrative of matters which drew attention from the cross itself.

Besides the store-house and Makola's hut, there was only one large building in the cleared ground of the station. . . . There was also another dwelling-place some distance away from the buildings. In it, under a tall cross much out of the perpendicular, slept the man who had seen the beginning of all this. . . .

Carlier went out and replanted the cross firmly. "It used to make me squint whenever I walked that way," he explained to Kayerts. . . . So I just planted it upright. And solid, I promise you. I suspended myself with both hands to the cross-piece. Not a move." *

In the first paragraph is only Conrad's habitual irony; in the second, only one more of many evidences of Carlier's erratic puttering. Yet the two mentions have rooted the cross firmly in the reader's mind. It is there, ready to serve its sinister final purpose.

For a beginner whose stories have a habit of sagging in the middle, a first step in improvement is the analysis of some story or part of story not his own, with an eye not only to the presence of repetitions but also to how they are fitted into the narrative. In the following paragraphs, for example, what are the points which repetition emphasizes? Are the repetitions numerous enough, varied enough, clearly directed enough? Do they avoid monotony?

* From *Tales of Unrest*, by Joseph Conrad. Copyright, 1898, 1920, by Doubleday, Doran and Company, Inc.

The man who had not wanted to come—his name was Rinton Clarke—opened the door of his shingle cabin and looked down across the valley. It was very early, but the sun was rising and through the river fog he could see the town and the grey bay beyond widening to meet the ocean in a line of tossing white. For a moment the beauty of it caught at his breath and his lungs filled in a quick gasp of pleasure. Then his face relaxed to its accustomed quiet and his shoulders again fell forward.

He left the door ajar and set about the preparation for his morning journey into the town. For four baffled years he had lived there on the hill's crest above Monterey, unoccupied, quite alone. No sunrise, no shifting of shades and colors could win him now from his habit of resentment. As he left the house he glanced again at the bay, grown purple in the advancing light, and scowled his tribute to it, much as a captured Moor might have paid tribute to the vestments of the inquisition priest. Then with his eyes on the ground he took the footpath down to the town.

There was only one house in the half mile between his own and the opening of the first street. As he came near it he checked his pace and, taking out his pocketknife, struck sharply two or three times on the top strand of the barbed wire fence surrounding it. Almost at once a girl came out on the porch and answered the summons by running down the path to the gate.

"You're early," she hailed him.

"I didn't think you'd be up," he acknowledged, "I only tried it to see. I couldn't sleep any longer."

"I didn't want to lie in bed any longer either," she amended the statement. "I'm just up, but I can't stay in the house. Isn't it glorious?"

"It is a beautiful day," the man admitted. "I suppose it will be like every other day, though, interminably long and end in a grey evening."

The girl looked up at him quickly. "You are worse?"

"Not worse. It's an anniversary, that's all. I've been here four years today—four years waste lumber." He smiled wryly at her.

"But why should one bother? Go on in and get your breakfast.
I'm going down for mine."

He nodded to her and strode on down the path. It troubled him
a little that, looking back, he saw her returning slowly, droopingly,
towards the house. He reproached himself perfunctorily.

"A part of my curse. I'd much better let her alone." But in a
moment his solicitude had veered back to self-pity. He could
have nothing that was granted to other men, he could touch nothing—

So much, then, for other people's stories. Now, what of
your own? There the story lies, written, in front of you.
What are the points—in action, in plot, in setting—on which
you mean to bear down? You have, let us say, a nagging
father as a main figure in the story. He is well-to-do, liberal,
devoted to his three daughters, but he cannot even momentarily leave them to their own untroubled devices. You pro-
pose to have his shortcoming held up dramatically before
him, to have him recognize it, determine on reformation,
attempt reformation, then slip back to his earlier habit. At
the end, he is to be in the same rut as at the beginning.

For the display of that one characteristic can you find
ten probable incidents? Are they incidents possible to a
father affectionate and well meaning? Do they fit to the economic and social standing you have given him? Should he
nag all the children equally? Should all of them offer the
same response? And what two other pieces of knowledge
concerning the family do you have to have before any of
the questions just asked can be answered?

One writer, dealing with such a father, made seven out of
ten incidents turn upon the father's forbidding his children

to do some one thing which all three wanted to do. He had, that is, not seven incidents but one incident seven times shown, though in slightly different dress.

Every reader of amateurs' stories has come across examples in which the incidents used had no intrinsic likeness, led to no end. These are hopeless. Where, however, as in the summary just given, there is a coherent idea to be developed, then the development of action appropriate to that idea is a matter chiefly of labor. This labor, this scrutiny and testing and fitting together of possible happenings, is exactly what the beginner oftenest refuses to do. When the excitement of having discovered a story is past, his mind goes no farther. To make it go farther, to center it on the search for interpretive action is something he feels to be beyond his powers. Often he is right. His mind, unaccustomed to discipline, cannot be commanded. But if his writing is to be other than spasmodic, his mind must sooner or later be brought under the control of his will. One way for bringing it under is to set it searching for relevant incidents. The searching, of course, is useless unless each resulting incident is honestly examined. Because all minds, but especially the minds of writers, are expert at avoiding effort, some of the forms of examination likely to prove useful are suggested below.

Using the excerpts from *A Jury of her Peers* as your guide, collect from your own once-written story, in mind or on paper, the whole group of incidents meant to enforce one idea. Does each one really tell on that idea? How many are there? When immediately juxtaposed, are they boringly similar either in happening or in wording?

Does each of your series of incidents fit to the external

conditions—the wealth or poverty, the social standing, the family background—of your characters?

Are the incidents chosen of varying importance, or are they all of approximately the same importance?

Does any one of them introduce a discordant, an unintended, idea into the reader's mind? If, for example, out of five incidents showing the heroine losing her temper, three show her losing it because of an irritation caused by one member of her household, is the suggestion thus given an intentional one, one having to do with the whole course of the story? Or has it slipped in only because repetitive incidents tend to be repetitive in form as well as in substance?

IV

Time

"Once upon a time—"

Suggested Reading

CRANE, STEPHEN. "The Open Boat," in *The Red Badge of Courage and Other Stories*. Boston: Houghton, Mifflin and Company.

BALDWIN, JAMES. "This Morning, This Evening, So Soon." *The Atlantic,* September 1960.

GRAU, SHIRLEY ANN. "The Empty Night." *The Atlantic,* May 1962.

JAMES, HENRY. "Four Meetings," in *Novels and Tales of Henry James*. New York: Charles Scribner's Sons.

DAHL, ROALD. "Mrs. Bixby and the Colonel's Coat," in *Kiss Kiss*. New York: Alfred A. Knopf.

FAULKNER, WILLIAM. "Wash," in *Collected Stories of William Faulkner.* New York: Random House.

STEGNER, WALLACE. "The Double Corner," in *The Women on the Wall*. New York: The Viking Press, Compass Books.

Time

I

SIT down with a group of six people who are telling anec-
dotes and you will notice that at least five out of six, and
more frequently the whole six, begin their recitals by the
mention of time. "I was going over to the store yesterday . . ." "A funny thing happened the other night. It was
just after I'd turned out the light; it couldn't have been more
than eleven . . ." Even recapitulations of meditations and
mental conclusions are given a time placing. "While I was
getting breakfast this morning, I was thinking . . ." "I
hadn't heard from him for a month, and I decided . . ."

Time is the inescapable factor in narrative, whether oral
or written. It is so because it is also inescapable in life. The
habit of thought bred by living carries over to both writer
and reader. If, in life, we let go of our time leading-string
even for a moment, the result is confusion. If we let go of
it in a story, the result is confusion too, the reader's confusion. What so overmasteringly controls existence cannot
fail to control fiction; and in the writing of fiction, the
treatment of time—the uses made of it for bringing out the
author's intent in a story—are among the none too numerous really learnable things.

The first thing to be learned is this: Unless the writer is
trying to exhibit confusion, the time of a happening in the

story and the intervals between happening and happening must be kept clear in the reader's mind. Every happening has not only a time of its own but also a time relation to other happenings. What these relations are, it is essential to show.

The easiest way of showing is, of course, by mention of exact time periods.

1. We left the house a few minutes after noon. It was three when we got to Santa Fé; we were driving pretty fast. Nancy wanted to stay there, but we argued her out of it. We did stop, though, for coffee and sandwiches. It must have been about five when we started up the Picuris hill. That's where the trouble came. The sun was pretty nearly down. Every time we made a turn, I had to use one hand to shade my eyes, and going round those curves one-handed—

2. They had a fine first day of sailing weather but after that . . . a light wind directly in their eye and they hung in the wide mouth of the Bay . . . longer than Donald liked . . . They pumped an hour a day . . . In five days' time they were not a hundred and fifty miles on their way . . . One day there was hardly any wind . . . at the next dawning the northeaster was here . . . by noon that day the Mary Jane was running under reefed sails . . . At dusk he thought to heave her to . . . That night was long and cold . . . When day broke feebly, the wind had become a gale . . . The dawn was gray . . . An hour after daylight Pat took the wheel . . .

—Ben Ames Williams, "The High Heart" *

A speaker habitually locates his time with something of the exactness shown in these two paragraphs, one of them by an amateur, the other by a practised professional hand.

* In the *Saturday Evening Post*, December 25, 1937. Used by permission of Harold Ober, author's representative.

A beginner, however, is likely to be oppressed by the frequency with which his time markers appear. "It was noon . . . ten o'clock . . . the next morning . . . a week later . . . the afternoon before"—to his own ears at least, the story is made up of identifying time statements. From some of them he tries to escape by circumlocutions, but as he proceeds with his writing, he usually discovers that the plainest time statement is the least obtrusive. A good deal is to be said for the definiteness of Genesis, which is also the definiteness of numbers of excellent stories. Witness John Russell in *The Fourth Man.*

But at sunrise, as if some spell had been raised by the clang of that great copper gong in the east . . . Under the heat of the day . . . By the middle of the afternoon . . . when the wind fell at sunset . . . through that long clear night of stars . . . It was an evil dawning . . .

The very simplicity of the wording renders it inconspicuous, and the reader is never at a loss for the progress of the tragic drama he watches.

When, in spite of plainness, mentions of time do stand out obtrusively, the difficulty is less often with the mentions themselves than with the planning of the story which contains them. A frequent reason for flocks of "the next minute," "the following afternoon," "when he saw her a week later—" is that the writer has not yet sufficiently labored out the arrangement of happenings in his narrative. Tags of action drift in which either are useless and so should have been left out entirely or else should have been brought into relation with events more important.

Occasionally, of course, it is the time markers themselves

which are important—important for themselves, since passage of time is a crucial event in the story.

The next day she passed him in the driveway but without speaking. On Saturday he saw her with her mother, standing looking in a window on Oak Street. In the week following, he had three hungry glimpses—on Sunday on her way to church; on Monday when she came out bareheaded into the garden—

Here not the glimpses but the spacing of the glimpses is meant for the reader's remembrance. So is the spacing in Lawrence Kirk's *Study in Black and White,* where the menu instead of the clock gives readers their understanding of the time a change of mind requires.

That was his opinion while they were eating the sole meuniére. Later on, when a wing of pheasant was on his plate, he had changed his mind. . . . When the table was being cleared for dessert, he was still of the same opinion . . .

Tracing back over his own story, a writer will find "When did it happen?" a question as useful for pulling the body of the story into shape as "Why did it happen?" is useful for helping him to decide whether or not he has a story at all.

II

John L. Doughty, 322 Frein Street, was arrested at his home yesterday on a charge of embezzlement. Doughty, who has been for twenty-nine years an employe of the San Francisco branch of the Western Fidelity Company, is alleged to have admitted that, since last August, he has three times altered his books to cover peculations. Walter Harris, manager of the San Francisco branch, stated that there was no evidence of irregularity on

Doughty's part earlier than August. "He was one of our most trusted employes," Harris said, "and was within two years of his pension. I cannot explain his action."

Walter Harris, manager, is fortunate. So is the reporter. Neither has to explain. The story writer must. If his story of John Doughty, embezzler, is to excite belief, it must make clear to the reader two things—first, why, after long and seemingly honest service, Doughty became an embezzler; and second, why his embezzlement began upon a certain day.

Keeping time clear, that is, is only one, and the easier to fulfill, of two time requirements. The second requirement is that, within the story, the time setting of a happening must allow for both the general causes—why it happens at all—and the immediately inciting cause which accounts for its happening at a particular time. The reader requires to know what pressures, working perhaps through years, undermined Doughty's integrity. Quite as much he requires to know too what final pressure incited action on the one occasion—why it was the fourth of August, not the fifth, not the third, which witnessed the final crumbling of his honesty. In life, the reason for this final crumbling, the initial reasons for dishonesty at all, may remain hidden. Even Doughty himself may have only the dimmest apprehension of them. In the story, it is the writer's obligation to bring them into view. Always, the reader of a story requires to be informed in one degree or another of the reason for a thing's happening. Always he requires to know not only why it happened, but also why it happened at one particular instant instead of another. A reason there always is, and the difference between the working of this necessity in life and in fiction is only that in fiction both reasons are brought into view. If they are not, there is probability almost to the point of certainty that readers will remain unconvinced and therefore uninterested.

In the amateur's story, inciting cause more often than general cause is the one insufficiently stated. It is worth noting, therefore, that the two are not necessarily identical or even obviously related. With John Doughty, the general causes for his act, whether in life or in the story, may go back to his childhood, to the examples set him by his parents. The inciting cause, on the other hand, the impetus leading to immediate action, is located at some one definite time point. Jack London's *To Build a Fire* is one of many illustrations of this difference. The story deals with a man's death on an Alaskan trail. The general causes for the dilemma which leads to death are the man's folly in having started out alone in sub-zero weather and, beyond that, his unimaginative obstinacy. The inciting cause is one particular misstep which sends him floundering through thin ice into an airhole. In Rose Wilder Lane's *Innocence,* a Northern family attempts to establish itself among hostile Southern neighbors. The general cause for their failure is the virulent enmity of those neighbors—an enmity displayed time after time before they are finally driven out. The inciting cause—the reason for their flight's taking place on one especial night—is that a few hours earlier they have barely frustrated an attempt to poison their only child.

In both these instances, the inciting cause is of considerable weight. It need not be, but, small or large, it must always be a specific thing, must always therefore occur at a

specific time; always, too, it must mirror exactly whate
the general causes have made clear. In actual happenir.
Jack London's hero might have died from slipping over ¿
cliff, from an attack of wild animals; the family in *Innocence* might have been driven from their farm because frost
or flood, added to hostile neighbors, defeated them. Under
such a change, though, either story falls to pieces.

Either general causes or inciting cause being insufficient,
a story is sure to suffer. Formulas are dangerous, but there
is one which might profitably be learned by heart. It is this:

> *General causes plus inciting cause should be equal
> to effect.*

Or, turned the other way round,

> *Effect is the sum of general causes plus inciting cause.*

The sum. Not less. Not greater. An avalanche of misfortune which leaves no evident scar on the soul of the character
concerned—causes outweigh effect. The financially embar-
rassed hero playing golf with a stranger and being asked
offhand to accept a managership—effect tips the beam too
far.

Possibility, of course, is not in question here. Most of us
have known chameleon creatures who took no permanent
color from experience. All of us have witnessed success or
failure arriving by what, so far as we could see, was pure
accident. In life, anything may happen; in fiction, only
those things endowed with credibility. And in fiction—to
say it yet one more time—happenings cannot be credible

ct balance at least momentarily in the

too if general causes, however sufficient in
are spread over what seems to the reader an
.e time period—one shorter than observation has
. him is needed for the alteration involved; one longer
.n he believes the situation or emotion presented could
sustain. Whether his belief is right—if "right" can be used
in such a connection—is of no importance. A storyteller's
business is so to space his happenings as to avoid the raising
of doubts. "Plausibility is the morality of fiction."

There was a time in writing when instantaneous destruction of character, instantaneous upspringing of emotion, instantaneous conversions, were in fashion. There may be such
a time again, but at the moment they are out of fashion. In
any realistic story, the implication, even if not the actual
presentation, of lapses of time is needed to convince a reader
that an honest man has become a rogue, a rogue an honest
man, and so following. *The Great Stone Face,* known to
every reader, makes the growth of Ernest's saintliness spread
from childhood to old age. *The Dark Fleece,* Hergesheimer's
story of the homecoming forty-niner and his New England
village, gives to the returned Jason fifteen years of absence
to account for his changes in character and outlook. In
*Miss Letitia's Profession,** the author presents his heroine
with twenty-three years of odd jobs to temper the iron of
her resolution, and fourteen years after that to reach a mod-
erate fame—and mentions each time a specific date.

* By Lupton A. Wilkinson. In the *North American Review,* July, 1934.
Used by permission of The Editors.

Miss Letitia saw the panic of 1897 wipe the investments as blank as the paper that reposed so long in her brother's typewriter. Shuddering a little, she took in sewing. . . . Miss Letitia sewed in and sewed out. The cottage sprouted a lopsided mortgage. In 1907 Rodney's salary was raised to thirty dollars. . . . One day—it must have been about 1920—

Time—time in plenty—is the reconciling element for almost any vital change in character or in placing. Readers' doubts on the score of possibility are destroyed by the passage of years before they are fully formed. On the other hand, brittle situations, emotions ordinarily evanescent, are instantly implausible unless they can be compressed into a limited number of days or weeks. There was once, in actuality, a grub-line rider who dropped in casually at a ranch for supper and stayed seven years. There have been, in life and in fiction, widows who, following their husbands' deaths, took for all time to crepe and silence and darkened bedrooms. Such static characters now are difficult to present. Psychology, psychoanalysis, the widening spheres of interest for all human beings, and especially for women, make such characters progressively more difficult. A week, a month, may frequently render plausible what a year-long interval puts quite out of court.

Ordinarily, the inexperienced writer meets more difficulty in the placing of his inciting cause than he does either in deciding on the whole extent of time he is to use or in the presenting of his general causes. Out of a dozen stories lacking in plausibility because of time treatment, fully three-fourths are faulty through the writer's having failed to make clear why action took place on a given day rather than why it took place at all. The reason for this is, of course, that general causes are tied up with the writer's conception of his story. They stand out in his mind whenever he thinks about it. A man broken by a nagging employer, a woman rising above the aching loneliness of a Dakota ranch—these are what his story is about, these are its substance. His inciting cause is neglected not only because a suitable happening is hard to find, but also because he sees no necessity for finding one. To his own mind, the general cause is all-sufficient. He has not brought himself to realize that general and inciting causes are separate things, are not necessarily even of the same external pattern. The general causes may go back to the hero's infancy, spread through his life, begin earlier than his life in the lives of his parents and grandparents. The inciting cause, the specific push to action, is one happening, placed at one definite time point.

Everything had been as usual that morning—the early breakfast, Frampton's sleepy departure for work, her own mechanical gathering up of the dishes. Then, suddenly—Ruth never knew how—she was outside the door, she was headed towards the road, towards freedom—

No hand but an awkward one could have written that paragraph. "Ruth never knew . . ." "Somehow she felt . . ." "What impulse moved him was never clear . . ." These are phrases to be watched, signposts of sloppy thinking. The humorous stories of Saki, stripped as these are to their very skeletons, make excellent studies of causes both general and inciting. In *Ministers of Grace*, for example, the general causes are exhibited in the character of the Duke of Scaw, as explained in the opening paragraph, and in the nagging of his friend, as exhibited in the first two pages. The inciting cause is the particular form of expression chosen by the annoyed cabinet minister.

"No power of earth or Heaven is going to move us from our place till we choose to quit it. . . . No power of earth or . . ." *

If only the cabinet minister had not dared Heaven, he might have avoided a horrid fate. And there is something for a would-be writer to think about in the fact that, in Saki's hands, that fate did not overtake him on the first dare but on the second.

The Saki stories are examples too of the balance between effect and sum of causes—are all the better examples because of the extravagant impossibilities which make up their substance. *Tobermory, Mrs. Packletide's Tiger, The Lost Sanjak, Gabriel-Ernest*—nobody "believes," in the ordinary sense of the word, in what happens in any of these stories; in the special, more limited sense which applies to fiction, everybody believes. Effect has been exactly balanced, equals exactly the sum of the offered causes.

For realistic stories, the safest guide is, as always, actuality. Holding the pattern of the story up against life, can a writer justify to himself the things his characters do? Can he justify them under the conditions he has established? How would the sum of the causes he has shown act upon some person he knows? Would they make that person do what the character does? Would they make him do it at the same point in time? Ethan Frome, heading his sled towards the Great Oak, does so for reasons no reader can deny. The

* From *The Short Stories of Saki*, H. H. Munro. Copyright 1930. Published by The Viking Press, New York

general causes, spreading through his life and casting their shadows across all his future, the inciting cause of Mattie's nearness, her impending loss, her importunity—taken together, the sum of these things is adequate. So is it adequate with Pyecraft, bobbing about against the ceiling of his room. Again, no reader believes, no reader is meant to believe in the sense in which he believes the sun will rise, that Pyecraft loses weight without losing rotundity and so unwillingly comes to emulate a balloon. But general causes and inciting cause add up neatly together, reach the required sum. If there were a Pyecraft, if there were a recipe, then what H. G. Wells makes happen is what would happen. Holding a story up to life means holding it all up—the characters, the situation, the conditions attached to that situation.

But to fit any story, and especially a realistic one, against life while the story is still hot in the mind is all but impossible. The fitting is a process not to be neglected, but it is one belonging strictly to revision, and one which, at any stage, taxes a writer's intellectual honesty. In daily experience, general causes are often so blurred, special cause so insignificant, that a person may say in all sincerity, "I don't know what made me do it," "I don't know why I acted like that." There is no such comfortable retreat for the maker of an imaginary being. He has to know why his figures "acted like that," he has to make the reader share some fraction of his knowledge. Psychology—not the kind that sends white mice scampering through mazes but the kind that looks to self-and-neighbor analysis and so, at long last, to the analysis in his own mind of the characters in his story—is the necessity of every writer.

It has already been said that general causes and inciting

cause need not agree externally. Nonetheless, inciting cause must press upon the particular sore point, emphasize the particular strength or weakness, which general causes have made evident. Somewhere in the shipwreck scene in *Ben Hur,* Lew Wallace pauses to philosophize upon his hero's escape.

> Beyond doubt every experience in life is useful to us. Where got Ben Hur the mighty muscles which saved him now? Where save in the galleys when he toiled as a slave at his oar?

Such a relation, whether for the salvation of the character or for his destruction, inciting cause bears to general ones. *Ethan Frome* is an exemplar here too. Ethan's life has been a slow starvation, an unavoidable surrender to meagerness, to querulous age and ugliness. Mattie is the antithesis of these things. Just as, in one crisis in the story, it is her expression of love for him which is the inciting cause, so in another it is her flushed prettiness.

But though the one cause is spiritually related to the others and is the final incitement to action, it does not therefore, as has already been pointed out, have to have weight in itself. Any examination of writing verifies this, and quite as much any examination of living. A neurotic, sure the world despises him, is driven to suicide by a thing so small as a child's scowling at him on the street. If the general causes for his condition have been adequately shown, then the special cause is all-sufficient, remains all-sufficient so long as it bears upon his own particular hurt.

Lack of this bearing is what usually makes impossible the lifting over into fiction of pieces of life as they stand. Rearrangement, extraction of the interpretive from beneath the obvious, is nearly always needed. A man may live next door to a caddish neighbor, hate him with a violence pushing towards murder, and yet be saved from murder by his firm's sending him to another town. That, however, is either not a story at all or is the story of something other than the hate of the two men—of some special effect of hate upon the hater, of some special emergence of his philosophy. So far as the men are concerned, the sequence of events in time—the cause and effect relation—is broken, and no story appears.

III

The place where a beginner at writing is most readily impressed with the importance of time treatment is usually in the individual passage. Usually, too, he recognizes its importance in the writing of others long before he can apply the results of the recognition to his own work. Consider the two paragraphs set below.

1. I had been waiting close to the telephone ever since five o'clock, expecting him to call as he had said he would. By the time the clock struck seven, I was in an agony of apprehension and impatience, my pride almost subdued to the point of calling him myself.

2. This is the last time I'll look at the clock. I will not look at it again. It's ten minutes past seven. He said he would telephone at five o'clock. "I'll call you at five, darling." I think that's where he said "darling." I'm almost sure he said it there. I know he called me "darling" twice, and the other time was when he said goodbye. "Goodbye, darling." He was busy, and he can't say much at the office, but he called me "darling" twice. He couldn't have minded my calling up. I know you shouldn't keep telephoning them . . . I know they don't like that. When you do that,

they know you are thinking about them and wanting them, and
that makes them hate you. But I hadn't talked to him in three
days . . . not in three days. And all I did was ask him how he
was; it was just the way anybody might have called him up. He
couldn't have minded that. He couldn't have thought I was both-
ering him. "No, of course not," he said. And he said he'd telephone me. He didn't have to say that. I didn't ask him to, truly
I didn't. I'm sure I didn't. I don't think he'd say he'd telephone
me, and then just never do it. Please don't let him do that, God.
Please don't.

—Dorothy Parker, "A Telephone Call" *

So far as the information given to the reader is concerned,
the first of these passages says as much as the second. It says,
indeed, rather more, for it carries the situation almost to its
conclusion. What it does not say, though—what it implicitly
denies—is that the time period presented is of importance.
In the latter passage, that importance is made obvious. By
sheer bulk of words as well as by their placing and content,
the reader is made to pause. Recognition and emotional response follow the pause, are dependent on it.

The surest means a writer has of impressing on his readers
that one passage is to be remembered, that another is no
more than a bridge from one high point to the next, is his
treatment of time. And time, of course, means space; in
writing, it can mean nothing else. A year collapsed into a
line, a minute expanded to a page—it is the minute that is
memorable. What is to hold attention or to excite emotion
requires length, either in itself or in the passages immediately
around it. What is only or chiefly for transition or for the
conveying of information is crowded into summary.

* From *Laments for the Living*, by Dorothy Parker. Copyright 1930.
Published by The Viking Press Inc., New York

 1. The wolves, first one and then another, came on stealthily towards the boy.

 2. The stealthy, approaching shadow crept a yard nearer, then paused to lift a grey muzzle and sniff the air. The second wolf, with slobbering jaws, turned to listen. . . . A minute passed . . .

 1. —— sat up, listening, thinking she had heard some one on the stairs.

 2. —— sat up, listening. Somewhere through the thick darkness a mosquito droned, a breeze stirred and fell. She could hear the light drag of a scrim curtain against the sill. Then she heard it again—the creak of a stairboard, a pause, then a second creak, a brushing noise as though a coat sleeve pressed against the wooden paneling.

For presenting his material, a writer has two time scales, no more. He may combine them—a sentence of summary, a scrap of dialogue, another sentence of summary—but they remain but two. And whichever he uses, it is never possible for him to present either a whole happening or a whole character. The most extensive, the most deliberate minute-to-minute presentation still is crowded with tiny elisions. If it were not, thirty seconds would fill a book. Where these elisions should be made, what to tell at length, what to minimize by summary telling, what to omit, are a writer's unending preoccupations. They are not the less his preoccupations through coming at last to be done largely by feel and without conscious choice.

That an important passage will usually be given minute-to-minute treatment, that informational passages will usually be summarized—these two things the veriest beginner already knows. But with every careful reading of somebody else's story, as well as with every attempt at a story of his own, the beginner discovers that these two things by no means make up all there is to be known about the uses of time in writing. Not what is the usual treatment of an important event, but how its importance may be momentarily concealed by summary; how, by minute-to-minute treatment, an unimportant passage may be given a factitious value or made the screen or the announcer of one to come; to what degree a recorded moment is affected by treatment not of the moment itself but of those preceding or following it—these are questions to which writers are forever seeking answers. If they are to write at all, time, for them, has to be elastic—has to be used as whole and half and quarter notes and rests are used by the pianist.

He broke off in his whistling. The lines under his hand tautened suddenly, then went slack as the horses came crowding back against the wagon. Ahead of them, so silently that no sound of it rose above the rush of the stream, there widened between bridge and approach a vertical gap. Deliberately, noiselessly, the middle span of the bridge, the empty pier beneath it, crumpled down to meet the water. For a fraction of a second Benson watched the gap. Then, in one complex movement, he had flung himself from the wagon and stumbled towards the lee side of the wreckage, the water roaring up to meet him.

Here, it is the important moment itself which is emphasized by detailed description. Often, though, the important moment cannot be prolonged. The act or speech or thought it chronicles comes and goes between the two ticks of a clock. To drag it out is to make it ridiculous. But to retard the story just before it, to retard just after, avoids absurdity and still gives to the moment the attention it requires.

"Fifteen," the elevator man announced. He clanged the door open, clanged it shut again. She was standing alone in the passage. Straight in front of her, a third the length of a city block away, a frosted glass door made a spot of dim yellowed light against the darkness of the walls. She could hear the elevator doors opening and shutting at higher floors, the sound softer with distance. Then the elevator was on its way down again. If it stopped at fifteen, if the man looked out and saw her standing there— Slowly, uncertainly, like a convalescent steadying herself for a first attempt at walking, she moved towards the dim light of the door.

The paragraph quoted is the opening one of the story. In it, retardation in advance of the moment serves the simplest of all its purposes. It warns the reader that something important lies beyond the closed door. It does that, and it does no more. There is no characterization, no description, no disclosure of the heroine's errand. She has come up in the elevator, she dreads going farther—that is all. Behind the door may wait a usurer, an injured husband, a surgeon, an alienated child. The reader does not know. What he does know is that, by dragging out the moment before it, the writer has cer..ered attention on the one to come.

In *The Night Hunter*, by Alexander Key, the young hero of the story has slipped out from a blockhouse besieged by Indians, to try to get meat for the hungry group inside. Those within the blockhouse hear two shots, one close upon the other.

Bush eased back upon the bar a trifle, thrust his face tight against the peephole. The moon had clouded again; the field stretching from the logs faded into an empty blackness a dozen feet away. He tried to visualize what was taking place somewhere a half mile beyond, tried to catch the first faint echo of a whistle that would tell him Ray was approaching. But he heard only the breathing of those around him and the scattered drops of rain promising a cloudburst. Thunder rolled like a regiment of drums. Lightning arched overhead, splitting the field with a white knife.*

The retardation here is not for reducing readers' suspense but for heightening it. Again, as in the earlier example, it is pause almost solely for the sake of pause. This time, though, the paragraph stands in the heart of the story, between one excitement and another. The reader, delayed by it, knows that important action is to follow the delay, as the spectator at a track meet knows that speed is to follow the crouched immobility of the runners.

But space in a story is always to be conserved. Only occasionally does a piece of retardation confine itself to one aim. The paragraph used to direct attention to a given moment can also convey information, delineate character, show the birth or death of an emotion, reiterate theme, enforce mood. In Stevenson's *Markheim,* one of the most useful of the retardations is that placed just before the moment of the murder.

The dealer stooped once more, this time to replace the glass upon the shelf, his thin blond hair falling over his eyes as he did so. Markheim moved a little nearer, with one hand in the pocket of his great-coat; he drew himself up and filled his lungs; at the same time, many different emotions were depicted together on his face—terror, horror, and resolve, fascination and a physical re-

* Used by the author's permission

pulsion; and through the haggard lift of his upper lip, his teeth looked out.

"This perhaps may suit," observed the dealer; and then, as he began to re-arise, Markheim bounded from behind his victim. The long skewerlike dagger flashed . . .

The physical manifestations here, taken one by one, are not especially individual. They might be those of any man nerving himself to murder. But though they might be any man's, they do nonetheless give the reader more than merely the pause which presages important action. Along with that, there is conveyed also an impression of Markheim—of his febrile tension and nervous instability—which bears upon his later action. Retardation, as it nearly always does, is serving a double purpose.

It serves a double purpose too, in Conrad's *The Secret Sharer,* in those three or four paragraphs which immediately precede the main event of the story—the mysterious appearance of a stranger at the ship's side, as though materialized from the sea. The paragraphs, too long for quoting, are worth thoughtful reading. What they accomplish is not only a pause in which time and place, the teller's love for the sea, his sense of an almost mystical relation to it are expressed, but also the retardation emphasizes in a reader's mind the sardonic contrast, essential to the story, between seeming safety and actual danger, between the placable face of nature and the animosity of man.

In *Spring Thaw,* the main figure in the story shoots a neighbor whom he had forbidden to set foot on his land.

The body of the shot man was pressed against the wire of the fence. The barbs sustained it for a moment, then, with a little zirr of torn clothing, it slumped down on the snow. Jennings dropped the barrel of his rifle, swung round and strode towards his cabin. He was not cold any longer. He flung his weapon up on its rack in a glow of satisfaction. O'Farrell thought he wouldn't shoot? Well, he'd shown him! He'd show any man. He guessed the place was his! Any man try to come on his place— He began moving about, putting the room to rights, replenishing the store of shavings in the woodbox. It occurred to him presently that he was thirsty, mouth dry, throat constricted. He turned towards the bench where he was accustomed to find the water-bucket and missing it, stopped to think. Sure enough! He'd been on his way to the spring when O'Farrell— He was aware of an immense reluctance at the thought of going outside for the bucket, at the vision of himself crossing the snowy field to the spring to fill it.

Retardation, coming after the event, allows the reader an interval for the fact of the shooting to sink in. But also the paragraph gives the cause for shooting, shows the ebbing of the rage which dictated the shot, the beginnings of fear. It has a triple use, not a single one.

The value of any retardation—its worth, its rightness— can, of course, be finally judged only in connection with the situation for which it makes an added emphasis. Thus far, the substance of the retardations quoted has concerned itself immediately with the actions or the reactions of the main figure in the narrative. In *Fifty Pounds,* by A. E. Coppard, the story stands still for nearly three pages while the heroine, sitting in a restaurant, listens to the talk of four clergymen at a neighboring table.

"I saw Carter yesterday," she heard one say. Lally liked listening to the conversation of strangers, and she had often wondered what clergymen talked about among themselves.

"What, Carter! Indeed! Nice fellow, Carter. How was he?"

"Carter loves preaching, you know!" cried a third.
"Oh, yes, he loves preaching!"
"Ha, ha, ha, yes."
"Ha, ha, ha, oom."
"Awf'ly good preacher, though."
"Yes, he's awf'ly good."
"And he's awf'ly good at comic songs, too."
"Yes?"
"Yes."
Three glasses of water, a crumbling of bread, a silence suggestive of prayer . . . Very delicate and dainty in handling their food they were, very delicate and dainty.*

The speakers have not been in the story before, they do not enter it again. They have nothing to do with it. The purpose they serve—their vapid talk, their impious piety—is only to underscore the heroine's mood of disgust with life.

It was fearfully hot. She knew now why the night had been so dark. The sky was no longer blue, but a dead, level white; its surface was too even to give the effect of clouds; it was as though in the upper air the heat hung like a pall. There was no breeze and the sea, as odourless as the sky, was smooth and shining like the dye in a dyer's vat. The passengers were listless; when they walked round the deck they panted and beads of sweat broke out on their foreheads. They spoke in undertones. Something uncanny and disquieting brooded over the ship, and they could not bring themselves to laugh.

W. Somerset Maugham, "P. & O." **

Weather, temperature, scenery are agents of attested usefulness for retardation. Human moods are notably accessible

* Used by permission of the author, given through his representative, A. D. Peters.
** From *The Casuarina Tree*, by W. Somerset Maugham. Copyright, 1926, by Doubleday, Doran and Company, Inc.

to them. Landscape, in life or in fiction, takes its color from the onlooker's feelings. To a less degree, rain and sunshine, heat and cold do the same. But to the amateur, such uses of externals are dangerously easy, a temptation to fine writing, to retardation for the sake of displaying that fine writing.

1. She stood motionless, looking down at the waves. Grey, oily, beating, retreating, advancing only to be sucked back again, futile as life itself—

2. He waited, staring in front of him, his mind swept clean of thought. Years after, he could have sketched the least detail of the scene—the avenue of pines, their tops black against the hard blue sky, the sun in dusty bars across the road between them, the dizzy round of sparrows above the bushes—

Both the pathetic fallacy, in however attenuated a form, and the "he-always-remembered" passages are to be suspiciously regarded in the revision of any story. Out of its context, neither of the paragraphs above can be pronounced wrong, but both would require to be called into account while the story was still in review. Why did she stand? Why did he? Is the stress on either of them sufficient to meet the emotional demand made by the writer?

Still more suspect are retardations containing extraneous information. In *The Cavern*, the hero has led the girl he has seduced into the depths of a cave and there attempted her murder. Believing he is leaving her dead behind him, he feels his way towards the cave's entrance.

His hand met a rough formation. "What's that? I'll bet, by gosh, it's a stalactite. Is it growing up or down? Let's see. No, it's a stalagmite. A stalagmite goes up . . ."

There is much more to the soliloquy, but more is not needed to show its uselessness. Retardation is required and pressingly required, for the attempted murder has surprised the reader almost as much as the victim, but the content of the retardation has to fall within the scope of the story's interest.

The example here is an extreme one, but the special shortcoming it exhibits is common enough—the thrifty attempt to make use of bits of stowed-away knowledge, bits of fine writing, quirks of observation. It should be an article of belief underscored in the creed of all beginners that anything born before, or separate from, the story to which it is attached, is doubly suspect by reason of that separate birth. Notebooks are valuable in a variety of fashions, but so far as retardations are concerned, the material committed to them is committed for burial rather than for resurrection.

It is occasionally possible for retardation before and after important action to allow the action itself to be omitted.

He tiptoed across the office, opened with his own keys the door giving on the jail corridor, and let himself into the jail. The sleeping figure on the sofa did not stir as he passed. It was still lying inert and heavy breathing when he re-entered a quarter of an hour later. He crossed the room and seated himself in a neighboring armchair.

What happened in that quarter of an hour is what gives point to the entire story. Not till much later does the reader know what did happen, but he is in no danger of forgetting that some event of importance has been prepared for.

A writer who has read as carefully as he has tried to write is aware that there are occasions where entire elision of the important minute best serves the story's purpose, where no possible presentation answers effectively to the suspense built up. When Poe omitted that instant in which his hero saw the contents of the pit, when Conrad, in *Heart of Darkness,* blotted out the tiny interval of time during which the secret follower grappled with Kurtz, they were acting on this knowledge.

IV

Use of time in the individual passages of a story is, of course, only one side of the time problem. For every story, there is a decision to be made before writing begins. This is, how much time, roughly speaking, the whole story is to cover—whether a day, a year, a number of years. Is the writer to follow his imaginary persons through linked series of experiences, external or mental? Or is he to concentrate on some single, close-packed hour?

The decision may change as the story grows, but a decision in advance there can hardly fail to be. And whatever it is, the maker of it finds one condition always with him. No matter how long the period to be presented, it is never long enough. Essential material lies always outside it, has somehow to be fitted in. The counsel from *Alice,* "Begin at the beginning and tell till you come to the end" is counsel any writer would like to follow, but, attempted, it proves itself the twin to that other sensible-sounding, senseless precept, "Put first things first." What is "first?" Where is an action's beginning? Romeo's eyes meet Juliet's, and love is born. But write the record of that love, and Montague and Capulet, nurses and cousins and priests, come pressing in. Nothing stands clear. The writer's dilemma here is like that of a marine botanist collecting on an ocean beach. He sees his specimen at the bottom of the tide pool—sees it, perfect in form, ready for preservation. He thrusts down careful fingers, raises it—and the whole floor of the pool comes too, scores of feeder roots, hundreds of parasites. How to keep the specimen, discard the useless attachments—

To do so with a story, a writer carries on two parallel processes. One is the separating of his chosen time from the rest of time in which it lies embedded. The other is the preserving or the re-attaching of past time's relevant fragments. As concerns the process of separation, it is axiomatic, as has been already pointed out, that what can be actually shown in a story is of the briefest. A story, whether it cover a year or an hour, is either a summary leading to some high minute or else a series of high minutes tied together by summaries. It is axiomatic, too, that the shorter the time elapsing between opening sentence and closing one, the easier the story will be to write.

The easier to write; not necessarily the easier to read. What readers' interest comes from ordinarily is concern for the persons in a story, and each of these is inevitably the sum of his past. A naked hour, then, standing without reference to that past, leaves little room for interest. Freeing it means no more than finding ways of reducing, in actual number or in space used, the bits of needed information which lie behind it.

Short-time stories, those dealing with a day or less, fall into two groups. In the one, the writer is engaged in showing a typical hour in his characters' lives, a period which has been repeatedly duplicated in the past and will be in the future. In the other, his preoccupation is with a crucial hour.

The aims being opposite, so necessarily are the treatments.

Stories dealing with a typical hour can be briefly disposed of. They come as near as any fiction can to escaping from time difficulties altogether. Either they are cross-section stories, in which the writer is chiefly intent on showing events battering a passive hero, or they are mood stories, where the chief interest is in displaying how the hero's mood colors events. For either kind, one hour, one day, within very wide limits, is as good as another. In Katherine Mansfield's *Mr. Reginald Peacock's Day*, for example, the very point of the story is our certainty that the day before and the day after exhibit Mr. Peacock exactly as does the day described. Whether it is Mr. Peacock's response to his wife's waking him, or his greeting his small son, or his singing in his bath; whether it is the Duke's addressing him as "Peacock"—"quite as if he were one of themselves"—or the titled music pupil leaving her violets in his vase, the happening effects neither a change in, nor an added revelation of, Mr. Peacock's attitudes and emotions, nor does it show him meeting any crisis. The purpose of each is to display one foible, which same foible almost any hour of his life except a sleeping one would display with equal fidelity. There is, therefore, almost no lump of prior information to be dissolved within the story. A reference is included to Mr. Peacock's marriage—"She had caught him in a weak moment"—but it is a reference expressing no more than Mr. Peacock's opinion. In the same fashion, Katharine Brush's *Night Club* dispenses with the need for introduced background. Any night at the night club is as good, is as bad, as any other night; the unseeing eyes of the main character look on them all alike.

With the crucial hour, on the other hand, the position is

exactly reversed. The hour chosen is unlike those preceding it—more often than not, it is also unlike any other ever to occur in the life of the character displayed. The writer's necessity in presenting it is the necessity of foreshortening. The hour must stand far in the foreground, must loom large, and yet its threads of relation to other hours cannot be disregarded. Whatever the hero's reaction to this special one, his past provides the reasons for it—except, of course, in those situations, sharply limited in number, where the hero is Everyman. Cutting down the amount of information needed about the past and breaking up what is left so that it can be slid into the story unobtrusively—these two processes go usually into the shaping of any record of a crucial hour.

For detaching the hour from others, the surest ways are, as always, those borrowed straight from life. A special placing—ship, airplane, Pullman—makes superfluous much that a more permanent location would involve. A catastrophe does the same, since catastrophic hours are by their nature crucial hours.

The Reverend James Fessler awoke as if from sleep. He raised his head and strove to look about him. Instantly the unstable element on which he rested shifted its place, and he went down, gasping and struggling. He had risen and sunk again before the recollection of a boyhood spent on the Maine Coast came to his rescue. His arms drew down, fingers spread, to his sides, his head tilted, and, nose just above the surface of the water, his lightened body floated.

A main figure could not well be placed in circumstances bearing less upon his ordinary life. And yet it is that "Reverend" tying him to it which gives to the opening such interest as it has. In Richard Connell's *The Most Dangerous Game,* the hero falls overboard, swims to an island, and finds himself sharing it with a man-hunting host. In Stacy Aumonier's *A Source of Irritation,* the stolid English farmer is snatched from the weeding of his turnip field by a German airplane, spends his crucial hour in Belgium, and is returned to his turnip field when the hour is over. In either instance, we still need to know something of the hero's past and a good deal about his temperament or we should be very little interested in his escape in the one case or his return in the other, but the number of things we need to know is sensibly reduced by his violent displacement from accustomed surroundings.

The End of the Party, by Christopher Gerould, offers an example of another kind, showing how far the number of attaching threads may be reduced and yet how necessary are the few remaining. The story concerns itself with a group of four—two boys, two girls—driving towards home at three in the morning and at sixty-five miles an hour. The driver stoops to light a cigarette, the car swerves, strikes a man walking at the edge of the road. Its passengers, sick with apprehension, turn back and discover him to be dead. The hour stands quite alone. What has happened is finished, will not happen again, or at least not to the same people, not in the same fashion. But though it stands alone, interest in it depends not on the happening itself but on those to whom it happened. By the briefest of references, it has been made plain that three of the four unhappy youngsters involved are of good family, are not habitual roisterers. The amount of knowledge the reader has about them is of the slightest, but his having it is what changes the case from the general to the particular. Once made particular, it needs no more attachment. Vicariously, the reader himself, his son, his daughter has done that killing. His mind leaps forward to its consequences—consequences credible because just so the accident might have happened to him, pleasurable to contemplate because his experience is vicarious only.

But though dissociation by means of unusual location or catastrophe is a frequent means of reducing the needed lump of prior information and is a means easy to use, still such dissociations are limited to special kinds of stories, with no possibility of application to far the greater number. More important than either of them, then, is a third means also illustrated by the Gerould story. This is the placing of the main person or persons in a situation immediately comprehensible. Every reader's mind, like every writer's, is full of preconceptions based partly on experience, partly on earlier reading. When a story agrees with these preconceptions, it calls for only a minimum of explanation. When it runs counter to them, its doing so has to be justified. And preconceptions, whatever they may be, are not static. In 1933, a story opening " 'I've got a job again,' Newman told himself, marveling. His feet beat out the tune of it as he walked. 'I've got a job, I've got a job,' " demanded no reconstruction of the reader's preconceptions and therefore only the slightest of justifications by reference to the past. Ten years later, justification, perhaps paragraphs of it, would have been required.

The beginner's fondness for striking situations leads him frequently to disregard the fact that the great bulk of experience coincides with established conceptions instead of running counter to them.

"Beastly!" murmured Lady Agatha to herself in her well-bred British voice. "Positively foul! They could well make these places higher." She removed a bit of coal dust from her cheek, regarded the handkerchief with which the removal had been accomplished, and tried again to improve her cramped position in the coal bunker. Again the unrelenting ship's beam rapped her smartly.

So far, so good. But Lady Agatha must be accounted for in that bunker, must be convincingly got into it and probably got out of it, or no story results. The greater the incongruity between person and situation, the heavier the weight of explanation; the smaller, therefore, the possibility of making the story anything other than an accounting for that opening incongruity. Manuscript after manuscript has come to grief through its writer's having mistaken a striking opening situation for a story.

Granted, however, that, so far as is compatible with the writer's purpose, situation and person have been adjusted, still there remain cases, many of them, where the amount of that compatibility is not great. A writer's story is not just any story, it is the story that particular writer wants to write. When all the adjustments have been made to a short time scheme that can be made without destroying the story, there yet remain precedent facts that the reader must know. The difficulties faced in introducing these facts are common to both short-time and long-time stories, for in both, no matter how carefully a writer has chosen his opening point, no matter what the congruity between person and situation, nonetheless, he faces the question of how to crowd into his first paragraphs an extra ten years or so of his person's experience. Again and again in the course of revision, he finds himself with bits of information seemingly essential to his story and nowhere to dispose of them. In the passages set below are illustrated four varieties of disposal.

1. "This weather," thought Reggie Sheldon, pottering about in his compact hillside garden, "justifies the Los Angeles Chamber of Commerce." He raised his chunky form from the flower bed and leaned on the fence, straightening joints that no longer had the elasticity of youth. Just beyond the fence, a retaining wall kept the garden from tumbling into a dirt driveway, which disappeared around a sage-covered hill, only to reappear in the canyon below. Farther below, stretching into warm haziness, lay the disconnected mass of suburbs known as Los Angeles. Reggie knew by the mid-day calm that a cooling breeze would spring up in the afternoon. He turned, with a feeling of complacent well-being, and surveyed his handiwork. The garden was at last reaching the stage when he and Dena could enjoy it. From an ugly hillside cabin, surrounded by a wilderness of sage and sumac, they had gradually produced the pleasant cottage just visible in its setting of vines and shrubbery. They had succeeded rather well, Reggie thought, in their imitation of the little houses on the outskirts of their native city of Sydney; they should be very happy here in their life of modest retirement.

Reggie Sheldon's life had been both varied and interesting. From his earliest days, he had been a born showman. His career in Australia had begun as a professional swimmer and water polo player. Then he had managed boxers, staged a six-day bicycle race. At last he had found success as an actor. He not only gained success with the troupe, but also he met Dena, who was playing in stock. Reggie felt himself fortunate in having married not only an attractive woman, but one who stuck with him, uncomplaining, until they had amassed sufficient money for retirement. The past was now only a vague panorama in their memories, made distant by the move to America; and, having shaken off every vestige of theatrical glamor, Reggie and Dena were simple, kindly people, entertaining to each other and to their friends.

A large black sedan wormed its way up the canyon, stopping inquiringly at every intersection. Reggie leaned against the fence and followed it with his eyes . . .

2. On those rare occasions when Mr. Benson sat down to self-examination, there was one point on which his conscience troubled him. In most respects—as neighbor, as husband, as pattern of kindness to his four stepchildren—he could congratulate himself on a clear score, but precisely under the last item there stood recorded a secret annotation. In spite of kindness, in spite of labored efforts at affection, in his heart Benson knew he did not like the third of his wife's children.

3. "I can't!" Judith Worth said, sobbing. "I can't, mother! Why, he's old! Every time I see him it makes me shiver."

"It didn't make you shiver before Ted Carson came along," her mother reminded her crisply.

The two were seated on the balcony leading from their rooms, the picturesque tumult of an Italian town below them. They had been in Italy nearly three months, driven there, as Mrs. Worth now reminded herself bitterly, by the dangerous attentions of this same Ted Carson—attentions which, till his reappearance two weeks earlier, she had congratulated herself on Judith's having forgotten.

4. Young Druten drew a long breath. "I believe I remember it," he said. "Anyway I remember Mother bringing me here, and seeing old Fu Lin squatting below. . . . He died . . . and his body went back home in a first-class coffin." . . .

Stella Druten slipped her hand through her husband's arm . . . "It's strange, isn't it? . . . your father and Fu Lin's, then you and Fu Lin himself, and now Jimmie and little Charles . . . I wish they'd call him Fu Lin as well. That makes three generations. . . . How old were you both, honey?"

"I was six and Fu Lin was eight. . . . His father had told him to look after me. . . . He did it for the next twelve years at a stretch, right until I went to college."
—Margery Sharp, "The Second Step" *

The story from which the first excerpt is taken deals with the reappearance of a former suitor of Dena's, with his invitation to dinner, Reggie's discomfort at the dinner, and his relief at finding Dena unaffected by her one-time admirer's prosperity. This being the story, two things about its opening are evident—first, that three quarters of the explanatory material is inapposite; and second, that the remaining quarter may readily be more closely packed, made within the same space to tell much more than it now does. In contrast with the first excerpt, the second disposes of name, relationships, subject of the story, all within a dozen lines which need no explanatory accompaniment. Before the writing of his opening page, any beginner can afford to recall those time-honored requirements of the elementary composition class: time, place, person, cause made clear in the opening paragraph.

Prolonged exposition following a brief exchange of speech, as in the third excerpt, is not impossible—witness Kipling's *William the Conqueror* and many other stories. The escape it offers from difficulties, though, is one dangerously easy. A beginner is probably wise to avoid it till after other means of disposing of material have been tried and found impossible. In the fourth excerpt, dialogue is used not to provide an opening for paragraphs of information but itself to include

* In *Harper's Magazine*, June, 1934. Used by permission of The Editors

the information needed. If it cannot be used so, if solid lumps of statement must follow the exchange of a pair of speeches, then usually either the wrong opening point has been chosen or the story is still heavy with superfluous bits of the past.

Recognizing awkward time placings in other people's stories is rarely difficult. Finding the same awkwardnesses in your own, once they have lodged there, is to be accomplished only by planned scrutiny. A mass of explanatory material requires to be divided into its bits, each bit tried against the whole. Is it necessary? Or is it a fragment belonging actually not to the story but to the piece of life out of which the story was pried? The Reggie excerpt—an extreme example—furnishes a field for exploration in two directions. First, which pieces can be taken away without loss? Second, what was the writer's process of thought which made those pieces seem necessary to him?

V

As was said in the preceding section, the first preoccupation of the writer of a story covering twenty years is exactly what it would be if his story covered twenty minutes—that of finding an opening point which presses as close as possible to what he wants to tell and yet leaves only a manageable bundle of earlier happenings to be disposed of. "As close as possible," however, is an elastic direction. That "close" may be a year away or a lifetime away or many lifetimes. If it is, and especially if the story is to have many scenes, what can time treatment do to prevent scrappiness and dragging?

The prime requirement for a story of many scenes is, of course, that the scenes themselves be relevant. If they are not, if the writer is not fully sure of what his course of months or years is meant to say, then devices are only the bailing of a hopelessly leaky boat. But even when relevant, the scenes have still to be connected. No scene is worth minute-to-minute presentation which does not advance the main idea, whether plot or mood or characterization, for which the story is being written. And in the long-time story, the gaps are frequently as important as the presentations. "Next day," once stated, may be taken for granted. "After five years," whether stated or not, must convey to the reader the sense of five years' having gone.

The simplest way for underscoring time breaks are the mechanical ones. As was noted in Section II, Hergesheimer's *The Dark Fleece* allows for fifteen years prior to the story's opening. For the months to follow, the author divides this rather long short story into twenty-two sections, each headed by a Roman numeral. That signal of time's having passed is one no reader can miss; the amount of time intervening, however, differs from a stretch of weeks to bare seconds. Twice, it is no more than seconds; once, the time it takes for Olive Stanes to turn, to stare, to recognize her returned and less than half welcome lover; again, the time in which the echoes of a shouted word die on the air. The divisions, that is, do what they must always do if they are to be effective—they recognize the india-rubber quality of time and force that recognition home upon the reader. They mark too not only passage of time but passage of time plus completion of episode or passage of time plus shift in point of observation. And for either of these double purposes they are space-saving devices as well as time-marking ones.

Asterisks and double spacing serve somewhat less formally the same purpose as division into numbered sections. They are signals, all of them, which even the stupidest of readers cannot miss. Less mechanical but as certain in its effect is the repeated word or phrase. Scriptural illustrations and illustrations from children's stories come first to mind, but there are plenty as well in contemporary writing by no means intended for children—the "we pumped" in Conrad's *Youth;* the imitation of Scripture, "Now Lo begat Loz, and in his old age gave the sword to him. . . . And Loz begat Lod. And when Loz died, Lod took the sword"—in Lord Dunsany's *The Sword and the Idol.* Such markers are devices in the full sense of the word. They may be made at any stage in a story's career. More fundamentally a part of the story is the marking of time by means of recurrent, though slightly altered, incident. Kipling's *The Brushwood Boy* begins, "A child of three sat up in his crib and screamed at the top of his voice," the cause of his screaming being an over-vivid dream. That dream, its figures sometimes metamorphosed but never beyond recognition, is what binds together the scattered experiences of a quarter of a century.

Where scenes are unavoidably many, reminiscent telling will sometimes hold a narrative together. Conrad's *The Lagoon,* in which the listening white man hears the native tell the story of his life, is an example. The happenings of years are brought together, unified, by their presentation in one narrative at one given time and place, unified too by the repeated inclusion of the white listener in the story, the repeated returns to high points in the past. (The reminiscent telling of a story within a setting of narrative or exposition disconnected from it, the boxed story, is discussed under *Points of Observation*.) These various means, however, though useful for increasing the effect of a chosen time plan, are not means for the creating of that effect. Its creation is achieved only by repetition of central idea, by enforcement, scene by scene, of the main thought, the core of meaning, of the story. Cohesion comes from idea. It may, though, be destroyed by way of telling. The substance of his story, the thing he wants to say, may be clear in the writer's mind, and yet the parts of the story stand as separate as unwired fence posts. How to tie the parts together is the easier to see if we consider first how time ties together fragments of some individual life.

A story is to detail twenty years of a man's career—a career leading to his destruction. Through the years that you have watched some one of your neighbors pass from respectability to wastrelhood, what have been the steps of that descent? If you sum them up in "drink," "divorce," "dishonesty," or some such inclusive word, you are merely begging the question. What have you seen, or what, if the walls of his house and mind had been of glass, could you have seen, to differentiate one year from another? What would there have been to show those years either as steps or as desperate pausing places along his road?

Stories dealing with change of character or with its marked intensification can scarcely be other than long-time stories. It is daily experience that alteration in a human being is believable only after time has tested it. Fiction, then, cannot do otherwise than support what experience has established.

VI

Suggestions for the improvement of beginners' work have been scattered through this chapter and still other suggestions will have been drawn from study of the quoted passages. If, however, none of these has touched on your own difficulties, what should come next? If, reading your work over after it has grown cold, you find your high moments blundering past without announcement, your retardations turning to dead stops, what are you to do?

First for the high moments. The story being once completely written, read it over, making up your mind again, now that you see it all on paper before you, whether or not it has substance, whether it really is, and still is, the story you purposed to write. If it is and yet is feeble and formless in its actual writing, then one step towards possible improvement is to examine the minute-to-minute passages, questioning the content of each one. Why is this passage worth minute-to-minute presentation? Why is this one? Reduced in mind or on paper to a half-page summary, what do the three or four pages of direct treatment contribute to the whole? If they make a contribution, then is the same contribution made elsewhere, and is it worth being twice made? If it is, what variations are there in the tellings?

The high moments having been interrogated and some of them perhaps discarded or reduced to summary, the summaries themselves come into question. Reconsidered, read one after another by themselves, do the summaries actually tell all the story? Again and again in beginners' work they do. The minute-to-minute tellings are no more than addenda to them.

Walking towards the farm, he thought back over the five months he had been away, over all the hardships and disappointments of them, and how his feeling for Hilda had grown with every day. He had feared when he left that she might forget him in his absence, take up with some younger man, but now he was sure she had not, for the message which had reached him through her brother was reassuring. When finally he was inside the house and Hilda and he were alone, he was almost beside himself with joy, wanting to hold her in his arms, to kiss her, to tell her everything at once.

"Five months, Hilda! Has it seemed as long to you?"

His kiss stopped her answer.

"I thought about it all the way up here. How long it had been, I mean, and how I'd missed you. There was a lot to go through, too, a lot of hardships, but being away from you was the worst. I kept wondering if you'd forget me. I thought maybe some other man—"

"I'd promised you—"

"I know you had, but when I thought about all the younger men—and then when you sent me that message by your brother—"

It is obvious that the story runs thin. It would run less thin if specific happenings, set in time, were included in the dialogue or if the dialogue itself were less one-sided; even so, minute-to-minute telling and summary parallel each other far too closely, the one scarcely more than an echo of the other.

But when high scenes and summaries have alike been examined; when, so far as you can tell, important happenings have been given emphasis, informational material stowed away, duplications sheared off, and still the story is ineffective, it is time to ask questions of the retardations. Besides retarding just before or just after an important happening, does the passage do anything else? Does it introduce information? Explain character? Glance at the story's theme? These questions being answered, there remains the all-important one. Softly read aloud in conjunction with what goes before and after, does the retarding passage fit? Is its feel right? Not too long, not too short, not ornate, not conspicuously irrelevant? The capacity to feel about his story is better for any writer than the capacity to reason, but in a beginner's revisions, reason has frequently to precede feeling and beat a path for it.

It is, of course, harder for the writer of it than for any other person to see a story's faults. You will sometimes help yourself for future stories, though not for the one in process of writing, by making a written time plan, the plan showing the moment of each action, the moments or hours elapsing between one action and the next, the reasons for the intervals. For certain kinds of stories—detective stories, stories of intricate external action—such a time scheme is an excellent thing with which to begin, and is nearly always a useful test of the first draft. For stories not of these kinds, however, it is a last resort, a counsel of desperation. The written scheme may show you what to avoid another time, but it is likely to leave you with a dead story on your hands.

V

Points of Observation

When John and Thomas, for instance, are talking together there are
at least six personalities to be recognized as taking part in that dialogue . . .

Three Johns
1. The real John, known only to his Maker.
2. John's ideal John; never the real one, and often very unlike him.
3. Thomas's ideal John; never the real John, nor John's John, but often very unlike either.

Three Thomases
1. The real Thomas.
2. Thomas's ideal Thomas.
3. John's ideal Thomas.

—OLIVER WENDELL HOLMES,
The Autocrat of the Breakfast Table

Suggested Reading

UPDIKE, JOHN. "Pigeon Feathers," in *Pigeon Feathers and Other Stories*. New York: Alfred A. Knopf.

HALE, NANCY. "The Bubble," in *Stories from* The New Yorker, *1950 to 1960*. New York: Simon and Schuster.

WRIGHT, SYLVIA. "How to Work a Guest." *Harper's*, May 1962.

IRVING, WASHINGTON. "Rip Van Winkle," in various short-story collections.

MAUGHAM, W. SOMERSET. "The Letter," in *The Complete Short Stories of W. Somerset Maugham*. New York: Doubleday and Company.

USTINOV, PETER. "God and the State Railways." *The Atlantic*, August 1961.

ROSTEN, LEO. "Mr. K*A*P*L*A*N and the Glorious Pest," in *The Return of H*y*m*a*n K*a*p*l*a*n*. New York: Harper and Row.

CONNELL, EVAN S., JR. "The Fisherman from Chihuahua," in *Best Short Stories from* The Paris Review. New York: E. P. Dutton and Company.

Points of Observation

I

WHEN Washington Irving presents Rip Van Winkle returning from his sleep on the mountain, he makes the presentation thus:

He had now entered the skirts of the village. A troop of strange
children ran at his heels, hooting after him, and pointed at his gray
beard. The dogs, too, not one of which he recognized for an old
acquaintance, barked at him as he passed. The very village was
altered; it was larger and more populous. There were rows of
houses which he had never seen before, and those which had been
his familiar haunts had disappeared. Strange names were over the
doors—strange faces at the windows—everything was strange.
His mind now misgave him; he began to doubt whether both he
and the world around him were not bewitched. Surely this was his
native village, which he had left but the day before. There stood
the Kaatskill Mountains—there ran the silver Hudson at a distance—there was every hill and dale precisely as it had always
been—Rip was sorely perplexed—"That flagon last night,"
thought he, "has addled my poor head sadly."

In this passage Irving gives to the reader Rip's observa-
tions as he walks (strange names over the doors—strange
faces at the windows), Rip's conscious thoughts (that flagon
last night . . .), the author's summary of Rip's mood (his
mind now misgave him. . . . Rip was sorely perplexed).
Irving, that is, watches Rip from the outside, enters and

reads his mind, offers authorial interpretation of what is happening within him. He is in full possession of the figure he has made.

The three passages which follow chronicle the same scene but alter the point of observation.

1. He had now entered the skirts of the village. A troop of strange children ran at his heels, hooting after him and pointing at his gray beard. The dogs barked at him as he passed. He stared from house front to house front and up and down the length of the street. "Where am I?" he questioned at last to the nearest of the children. "There is the Hudson. There are the Kaatskills, just as I remember them, but this village is strange to me." The child did not answer, only drew farther back towards the great oak at the foot of the street.

2. He had now entered the skirts of the village. A child, standing at the edge of the road, saw his approach and turned to scamper up the street, frightened at his queer look. An old man of the mountain he seemed to the alarmed youngster, perhaps a troll, perhaps a crazy man escaped from some prison. Looking back at a safer distance, the child could see that the newcomer was staring about from side to side like a man wholly bewildered, while bolder children tagged at his heels, and dogs barked behind him.

3. He had now entered the skirts of the village. A troop of strange children ran at his heels, half delighted by his queerness, half afraid of it, themselves unaware that Rip's own unawareness of their presence held them back from tormenting him. He walked slowly, staring from side to side, bewildered, at unfamiliar housefronts. "That flagon last night," he told himself, sorely perplexed, "it has addled my poor head." The youngest of his pursuers, catching Rip's glance, began suddenly to cry, uncertain why he did so. An older brother, close on the stranger's heels, cast a "cry baby" back at the weakling, ashamed of such faint-heartedness within his own family.

In the first of these passages, the writer gets into nobody's mind, allows himself to tell only what could have been seen and heard by any favorably placed onlooker.

In the second, Rip is shown not from Rip's standpoint, nor yet openly from the author's, but as he appears to one of the other persons in the story.

In the third, the author is everywhere—outside Rip, in Rip's mind, in the minds of his followers, first collectively and then individually. He sees everything, hears everything, even recognizes emotions unrecognized by their possessors. He is omniscient.

And *Rip Van Winkle* could, of course, be told not only from these but from other points of observation. The ones here given, if carried through the story, would alter it but would not metamorphose it. Told with entrance only into the mind of a neighbor favorable to Dame Van Winkle, it would become another story. Told in the first person with Rip in the teller's role, scarcely a shred of the original would be left.

The same material, the same persons and time scheme may make a dozen different stories according to the point of observation on which the writer decides. Points of observation, that is, are not fixed by the material; they are fixed by the individual who deals with that material. Even if the figure presented is a man alone on a water-bound rock or a man inside a padded cell, he still can be considered from within or from without. Neither does a writer's first consideration of his subject nor even the first draft of his story fully decide the point from which he is to observe it. Dorothy Canfield Fisher explains in her very useful pamphlet, *How "Flint and Fire" Started and Grew:*

One detail of the mechanism remained to be arranged, and this ended by deciding the whole form of the story, and the first-person character of the recital. This was the question of just how it would have been materially possible for the bed-ridden old woman to break down the life-long barrier between her and her sister, and how she could have reached her effectively and forced her hand. I could see no way to manage this except by somehow transporting her bodily to the sister's house, so that she could not be put out on the road without public scandal. This transportation must be managed by some character not in the main action, as none of the persons involved would have been willing to help her to this. It looked like putting in another character just for that purpose, and of course he could not be put in without taking the time to make him plausible, human, understandable . . . and I had just left out that charming widower for lack of space. Well, why not make it a first-person story, and have the narrator be the one who takes Mrs. Purdon to her sister's? The narrator never needs to be explained, always seems sufficiently living and real by virtue of the supremely human act of so often saying "I."

Quite as often a story begun in the first person runs into obstacles and is changed to a third-person one. Or in third-person telling, the teller assumes omniscience, finds it clumsy, excludes it in favor of location within a single consciousness. For a beginner, the deliberate working over of a situation—the telling of it first from one, then from another, point of observation—is an exercise not to be neglected. Consider the following skeleton of a story, based on a set of circumstances which nearly every one has had opportunity to watch:

X, early a widow, has taught school to support herself and her one son, Y. After Y has finished college and found a small position, X is retired on a tiny pension. Pension and salary combined keep the family solvent. A year or two later—long enough so that his mother has grown accustomed to being in command of the household—Y falls in love. X's pension is not sufficient to permit of her establishing a home alone; Y's salary will not cover the expenses of a household unless the pension ekes it out. The three people concerned, all three well-bred, well-meaning, reasonably unselfish, talk the situation over and decide on a joint establishment. It is the only decision possible if Y's marriage is not to be indefinitely postponed. The story opens after the marriage.

The narrative may end in any of several ways, but its general course—the domestic rubs along the way, the unintended irritations, the attempts of both women to shield Y or to enlist him—these are things any writer can predicate. He can do so, not because he has seen the situation expressed in fiction but because he has watched it in life. What he cannot predicate, except as he finds the answer within himself, is from what point of observation it is best to treat the material. Turning it over in mind, he finds it may be told in any of the following fashions:

In the first person, with one of the three figures serving as "I."

In the first person, with "I" a neighbor, a relative, an old friend.

In the first person, with "I" in any of the roles named thus far, but distant in time from the events he is relating and so telling them reminiscently to illustrate some general principle.

In the third person, with access, on the writer's part, to one or two or all three of the minds concerned.

In the third person, with the writer arrogating to himself

omniscience, and knowing, therefore, not only what his characters think and feel but also why they so think or feel—what forgotten childhood influences, what inherited tendencies are in control of them.

In the third person, with, again, a neighbor, relative, old friend in the teller's role.

In the third person, with the events of the story refracted through the stream of consciousness of one of the characters.

In the third person, by means of external evidence only—such evidence as an invisible watcher, looking and listening, might collect.

All these possibilities are before a writer when he sits down to deal with the story of X and Y and Y's bride. All of them are before him when he attempts to think out his own story. In the paragraphs to follow let us analyze, and not for X and Y alone, what effect the use of one or another point of observation is likely to produce.

First for the stories told by "I": Alexander Botts distributing Earthworm tractors over the globe and relating in reports to his firm his version of the distribution, Dr. Watson playing Boswell to a Johnson more bizarre than the real Boswell dreamed of; Marlow looking back to the days of his first voyage—these are examples of the three "I" tellings named earlier.

A story told by the main figure in it has one outstanding advantage. It presents itself to the reader in a form to which verbal narrative has accustomed him. Like verbal narrative, it carries an extra weight of credibility. "I was there. I did it. It happened to me." It has, too, in common with all first person narratives, the advantage of a scope automatically limited. There is no question of whether or not to shift the point of observation; once taken, it is taken for the length of that particular narrative. There is thus an enforced elimination of material which lies outside the range of the teller's attention. There is a marked reduction of time difficulties, since the story must follow the movements of one person.

Against these advantages, though, are set heavy drawbacks. The first of these is that what reaches the reader does so only after passage through the mind of a person himself of main importance in the action he is recording. If the story is one of adventure, suspense is usually diminished. "I" seeking to land a crippled airplane, to escape from an explosion—we know that "I" did land, did escape.

A second drawback is frequently harder still to overcome. In a recent amateur story, the hero commented, "I faced the new danger with unshaken courage." The sentence illuminates a whole field barred to first-person telling. With the rarest exceptions, "I" cannot arrogate to himself courage, high-mindedness, exceptional intelligence—any of the major virtues. He cannot unless he does so with his tongue in his cheek or under circumstances which deny the claim in the moment of its making. A figure deep in the happenings of a story and yet its teller stands always to lose. Disorders of mind, flaws of temper, absurdities, delusions—for these he can be the chronicler and often is the only one who can. Where it is intended that the reader shall feel admiration for him, he cannot—not, at least, within the limits of the short story; the novel, with its greater scope, allows for a few exceptions. Where, on the other hand, pity or horror, irritation or amusement, is the emotion to be excited, first-person telling is often the most effective.

In Sherwood Anderson's *I'm a Fool*—"It was a hard jolt for me . . . Even yet sometimes when I think of it, I want to cry or swear or kick myself"—the "I" is disgustedly recounting the items of his own folly. In *Sentimental Rubbish,* by Roland Pertwee, the hero announces of himself:

I was never a man who believed in a lot of sentimental rubbish . . . I have tried to show him [his son] the value of reticence . . .

and proceeds to deny his claim in action as often as it is formulated in words. In both stories, the use of "I" brings the reader closer to the main figure, whether to the lad condemning his own quite understandable vanity, or to the father bent on disguising his tenderness towards an only son.

One other use of first-person telling by a main figure should not be entirely overlooked though it needs no more than mention. This is that telling in which the actor is actually not an individual at all, is instead a composite, is Everyman, set in circumstances to which all humans would react alike. *The Pit and the Pendulum,* discussed under REPETITION, is also a sufficient example here. Many of Poe's stories, or the stories of Ambrose Bierce, would serve as well.

The reminiscent story told in the first person may, of course, be told by either major or minor character. Told by a major one, the teller is, ordinarily, a character metamorphosed by time, one looking to a point so far behind him that the "I" who speaks, speaks of a being no longer himself, never to be so again, but known to him as no other can be. At first thought, this reminiscent "I" seems to have all the advantages with no outweighing drawbacks. The advantages are real—real enough to have made the form a favorite with numbers of writers. There is, though, one accompanying requirement which usually renders this point of observation difficult for a young writer. For the reminiscent story can proceed even less than others merely on related action plus explication of character. Looking back across life, it is essential for the teller to have learned something from life's passage. He must possess philosophy as well as recollection, and this philosophy must animate his narrative. Without it, there is no reason for his taking charge of the story.

The most frequent form of reminiscent telling is that which puts the main story inside a box or frame, giving to one "I" the seemingly disconnected opening, then passing on to another the actual relation.

I had known him for so long that I had all but forgotten the queer start of our friendship. I had never spoken of it—at first because I was too shy, later because I loved him, later still because it was gone from my mind. That evening, though, as we sat in our sodden bedroom, tired both of us from the long drag of the factory day—arm out, arm in, arm out again—he turned his head to look at me and, his eyes holding mine, I remembered. I could see him see me remember.

"Well, ask," he said after a little. "Ask, why don't you? I don't mind. It was like this . . ."

Thereafter the first "I" is gone, to emerge, if at all, only at the end, or for a semi-occasional sentence along the way, in order to keep the reader reminded that what he reads is being received from the lips of one of the actors.

It was our first night in camp—a camp in the heart of California redwoods. We had been hilarious on our way in that afternoon. We had been mirthful at sunset and mildly cheerful through the coming of dusk, but now, with full night around us, laughter halted. Moment by moment we drew closer to our spark of campfire, as ineffectual as a glowworm in the Catacombs, and oftener and oftener our eyes traveled unwillingly up from its small consolation to the looming tree shapes overhead and the funnel of sky that showed between.

"Looks like the shaft of a mine," Drury commented under his breath, lying back on the redwood needles and giving himself up to contemplation. "Looks like a tunnel tipped up on end. You know I was in an up-ended tunnel once . . ."

And the story is on, a story entirely intelligible by itself, having nothing to do with redwoods, nothing to do with camping, but echoing, if it is to be a successful one, the mood in which it has been inaugurated.

The simplest of all the uses of the box is its use as a space saver. Time, place, immediate circumstance, relation of hearer and teller may be packed into it with an alluring economy. Children's stories provide the best examples here, especially those which run in series, the little boy returning each time to the cabin or the nursery or the library for a new recital. Aside from this obvious use, however, are others which have nothing to do with space saving. Quotation sufficient to show both the content of a boxed story and the reason for the form of telling would require pages. Some examples, however—*Heart of Darkness, The Apple Tree, Bertran and Bimi*—are likely, one or all three, to be familiar to any would-be short story writer. In each, the main story is complete without the box and would be a compelling story if no box existed. Why, then, use one? What does the box add to, what does it subtract from, the material it encloses?

Thinking back over any set of boxed stories, most readers will pick out for themselves at least two contributions. These are that the box provides an incentive for the "I" to begin his story and that it establishes at the very beginning the central idea which is to bind the incidents together. In *Heart of Darkness,* Marlow, middle-aged, sits on the deck of an anchored yawl, watching the placid Thames at sunset.

"And this also," said Marlow suddenly, "has been one of the dark places of the earth. . . . I was thinking of very old times, when the Romans first came here. . . . Imagine the feelings of a commander of a fine—what d'ye call 'em?—trireme in the Mediterranean, ordered suddenly to the north. . . . Imagine him here —the very end of the world, a sea the color of lead, a sky the color of smoke, a kind of ship about as rigid as a concertina, and going up this river with stores, or orders, or what you like. . . . Land in a swamp, march through the woods, and in some inland post feel the savagery, the utter savagery, had closed round him—all that mysterious life of the wilderness that stirs in the forest, in the jungles, in the hearts of wild men. There's no initiation either into such mysteries. He has to live in the midst of the incomprehensible, which is also detestable. And it has a fascination, too, that goes to work on him. The growing regrets, the longing to escape, the powerless disgust, the surrender, the hate." *

The story which follows is the story of a twentieth-century darkness; of colonizers as rapacious as were the Romans and even less permanent; of one colonizer in especial, whose surrender to the abominable is the center of the

* From *Youth,* by Joseph Conrad. Copyright, 1903, by Doubleday, Doran and Company, Inc.

narrative. The comprehension needed for understanding his surrender, for that identification of self with the figure in a story which is a chief delight of fiction, is provided by the box. So too is the parallel between a first-century England and a twentieth-century Africa. The box, underlining the special meaning of the story, has a connection with it which is spiritual, not merely the connection of like circumstance or like place.

A second usefulness is that the placing of a box around the story affects the amount and sometimes the kind of emotion excited in the reader. On the one hand, it lessens the impact of over-hideousness (*Bertran and Bimi* is an example here) by interposing between it and the reader the veil not only of time but also of a second person's interpretation. Up to a given, though variable, point, readers take pleasure in the presentation of horror. The point where pleasure ceases is where the screen made up from time and distance and unlikeness to self becomes too tenuous to hold the horror off. The box is one means of keeping it pleasurably distant. On the other hand, it is possible for a box to enhance emotion by drawing a parallel between the prospective fate of the teller and that of a figure in the story. Or it may point not in the direction of teller's fate but of reader's—"Thus will it be with you too."

These things a box can do. What it may not do is to provide merely a starting point for a story or a refuge for some piece of rhetoric otherwise lost to the world.

It was our first night on shipboard. Five of us, strangers that morning, old friends now, were sitting on the upper deck of the *Rantolio*. Our deck chairs were drawn close together so that we could see each other's faces through the thin, fine, silvery fog which since sunset had wrapped itself round the ship.

"You know what this fog makes me think of?" Lintauer asked when a crack in the conversation gave him room to thrust in his question. "I was on a tramp steamer in the Mediterranean once—night just like this . . ."

The chances are against Lintauer. If nothing thicker than a fog, and a recollected fog at that, ties the box to what is to follow, the writer would probably do better to come out into the open and tell his story for its own worth. Telling a story inside a box is one of the most useful of experiments, but for a beginner it is likely to be an experiment only. In the hands of an amateur, the box itself, written, polished, repolished, loved by its writer, frequently proves more attractive than the story it encloses; frequently, too, it extends to that story only the thinnest of spiritual connections. It is a fairly safe rule, one to which the exceptions are few, that no story should be put inside a box unless the box comes to mind after the story or simultaneously with it, not before. Only a relation far more vital than mere likeness of place or coincidence of happening can justify a union.

"I must have a dance of some kind, you know," says Mr. Folair, addressing Nicholas Nickleby on the subject of the tragedy Nicholas is adapting to stage use. "There's nothing easier . . . You get the distressed lady and the little child and the devoted old servant into the poor lodgings, don't you? . . . 'Oh, Pierre,' says the distressed lady, 'would that I could shake off these painful thoughts! . . . Do you remember that dance, my honest friend, which, in happier days, you practised with this sweet angel? It never failed to calm my spirits then. Oh, let me see it once again before I die.'

There it is—cue for the band—*before I die*—and off we go."

A minor figure is often an easy one to use for first-person telling. The difficulties he presents are only those connected with his plausible introduction into the scenes he is to describe and those springing from the increased chance he offers for digression. If he is to be more than the casual introducer who, as in Kipling's *Plain Tales,* wanders in near the beginning and later is forgotten by his maker, the simplest of his uses is as the reader's representative, asking those questions and receiving that information that enables the reader to follow the action. Witness, for example, the redoubtable Sherlock Holmes in conversation with Dr. Watson.

"My room at The Cedars is a double-bedded one."
"The Cedars?"
"Yes, that is Mr. St. Clair's house. I am staying there while I conduct the inquiry."
"Where is it, then?"
"Near Lee, in Kent."
"You forget that I know nothing of the case."
"I shall just have time to tell you the facts—"

And the facts the reader requires for an understanding of the action to follow come forth, close-packed.

Another possible function of the teller is to enhance readers' emotions by exhibiting his own—"I ducked down behind the bushes as the thing came past me. I could hear it whimper, and every inch of my skin was gooseflesh and my heart thumped inside me like a drum"—and always he adds, as does any 'I,' a small extra touch of authenticity. "I saw him do it. I was there when it happened."

In neither of the two kinds of stories just mentioned does

the minor 'I' as teller add any new effect to the story. His presence allows for the giving of information, perhaps sharpens emotion, but it does not alter the quality of the emotion. It is possible, though, for 'I' to do far more. In William Allen White's *By the Rod of His Wrath*, the 'I' is not only himself and in a measure the reader, he is also the community, the whole outraged little Midwestern town, watching and abhorring the downward course of its richest citizen. The use of the 'I' changes the quality of the abhorrence from individual judgment to general. In Galsworthy's *The Man Who Kept His Form*, the 'I' begins as recorder only. The hero pursues his hard way, "keeps his form" through loss of fortune, his wife's desertion, his long war service, till at last, dropped from his earlier estate, old and ill, he sits in the rain on the seat of his unhired cab. The teller looks back, sees him there—and becomes interpreter as well as reporter.

He had resumed his driver's seat, and, through the rain, I saw him with a cigarette between his lips, and the lamplight shining on his lean profile. Very still he sat—symbol of that lost cause, gentility.

It is a conclusion which unifies the narrative, gives it significance and general application. The 'I' has taken no striking part in the action of the story, less even than Dr. Watson takes in Holmes' adventures, but his presence has altered the story's meaning.

A minor figure telling a story in his own person has roles in plenty aside from those illustrated—has almost as many possible roles as there are stories. And whenever his use is other than mere recording or the drawing out of information, his attitude towards events, his personality, his way of tell-ing, color the narrative. If they do not, he is no more than waste lumber in the story.

That he will be waste lumber is, of course, one of the dan-gers in dealing with him. First-person telling slides so lightly from time point to time point, shakes off so many of the re-strictions which pertain to "he," that a writer is tempted to use it without much thought of what the unobtrusive "I" con-tributes. Somewhere very early in the writing of a story, that contribution should be brought to mind, analyzed, weighed. Why should a neighbor, a son, a servant relate a set of hap-penings not especially his? To help in answering the ques-tion, let us turn again to X and Y and Y's bride. If their story is to be told by a neighbor, with whom does the neigh-bor sympathize? How does he get his information? Will getting it involve improbabilities not involved in a more impersonal telling? What kind of individual is this neighbor? Do his prejudices, his involved emotions, his special kind of temperament give to the story some value it otherwise would not have?

These are the questions we ask for the story of X and Y and Mrs. Y. For your own story, where they are always far harder to answer, they need to be asked and reasked. Even when the story has been born into mind as a first-person story, they still need asking. It may have been so born not because it will actually be helped by first-person telling but because of some oddity of speech of the teller's, some en-ticing opening scene. One way of testing the worth of first-person telling is to put yourself mentally into the position of a listener. Granted that the person, the time, and the place were those shown in the story, could you, the listener, accept the teller's narrative and be convinced by it? What would you get from the teller which third-person telling would not give? Would material be open to use with third-person telling which is barred by first-person? And is that material valuable? Easy transition from scene to scene being counted out, what does "I" add? Unless it adds something more than easy transition, a beginner at fiction is likely to be safer with "he."

II

As the girls crowd in or out of the factory gate you may hear the loud hum of the novelist's art in full play. One girl is relating aloud to a friend: " 'Well,' sez 'e, 'you come along 'o me or stop where y'are. Please yourself.' And so she gev it 'im straight. 'It's all off,' she sez, 'an' I'm goin' straight 'ome.' " That girl, you see, keeps close to drama. Her novel just gives you each character's most expressive speech. Therein it resembles *The Awkward Age* of Henry James, whom no factory girl could surpass in the nicety of his care to tell a story the right way.

But hear how another girl treats a similar theme . . . " 'E thinks to 'imself," says this girl, " 'we'd better know right off,' 'e thinks, 'who's master 'ere.' An' so 'e give 'er the office a bit stiff. 'Well,' thinks she, 'ain't I to 'ave my bit o' pride, same as 'im?' An' so she let 'im 'ave a fair nose-ender." This girl is a little sister of Dickens and of Tolstoy. She "goes behind" her characters *ad lib.* She assumes omniscience about their private thoughts.

But listen to a third girl's way of going to work on the tale: "So don't arsk me what 'appened. I'm only sayin' wot our 'Liza tol' me. Somethink orful, 'Liza sez it were. 'Im orf the deep end, wantin' to ply lor' and master to the gel, 's if they was married an' all; an' 'er as bad as 'im, the cat—" In this girl the sovereign instinct of Conrad, as a technician, is manifestly present. 'Liza is her Marlow. Her heart tells her, as Henry James's told him, that if she gives the story simply and wholly as it struck 'Liza, "the terms of this person's access to it and estimate of it contribute by some fine little law to intensification of interest."

—C. C. Montague, *A Writer's Notes on His Trade**

To the little sisters of Henry James, Dickens, and Conrad introduced in the quotation above, let us add one more. This is the little sister of Virginia Woolf, a sister who holds the whole story within her, sees it not as it appears to others nor yet as someone has told her about it, but only as it glimmers up from beneath the stream of her own consciousness. This fourth member having been added, we have in front of us the four ways in which third-person stories are told. There are stories told objectively; stories where events are submerged beneath the stream of consciousness; stories where the writer sees through the eyes, or goes in and out of the conscious mind, of one or more of his characters; stories where he allows himself the freedom—and the penalties—of omniscience.

The dealer, while he thus ran on in his dry and biting voice, had stooped to take the object from its place; and, as he had done so, a shock had passed through Markheim, a start both of hand and foot, a sudden leap of many tumultuous passions to the face. It passed as swiftly as it came, and left no trace beyond a certain trembling of the hand that now received the glass.

"A glass," he said hoarsely, and then paused, and repeated it more clearly. "A glass? For Christmas? Surely not!"

"And why not?" cried the dealer. "Why not a glass?"

Markheim was looking upon him with an indefinable expression. "You ask me why not?" he said. "Why look here—look in it—look at yourself! Do you like to see it? No! Nor I—nor any man."

* Published by Chatto and Windus, London. Excerpt used by permission of James B. Pinker and Son, author's agents.

The little man had jumped back when Markheim had so suddenly confronted him with the mirror; but now, perceiving there was nothing worse on hand, he chuckled. "Your future lady, sir, must be pretty hard favoured," said he.

—Robert Louis Stevenson, *Markheim*

Markheim, as every reader knows, is a study of the working of conscience. Precisely because it is, it is instructive to observe how much Stevenson succeeds in telling by means of externals. Markheim's emotions are recorded through the movements of his body, the changes in his face, not by entrance into his mind. What is set down could have been seen by any stranger peering through imperfectly closed shutters. *Miss Hinch,* by Henry Sydnor Harrison, is told throughout from a point of observation which is that of a conveniently located seeing eye, a conveniently located hearing ear, no more. The same is true almost throughout of Ernest Hemingway's *The Killers.* In Kipling's *At the End of the Passage,* from its opening sentence, "Four men theoretically entitled to life, liberty, and the pursuit of happiness, sat playing at whist," to its cryptic closing quotation, the observer's attitude is departed from only twice and then only briefly and for additions to readers' knowledge which are relatively unimportant.

Objective telling imposes on a writer a severe self-restraint. It is more closely hedged about than any "I" relation, since "I" can always include his speculations along with what he chronicles. For many stories, for some parts of most stories, objective telling is impossible. But where a story can be so told, it is a powerful aid to effectiveness; information comes—or seems to come—in the way that it comes habitually in life, by means of eye and ear. The writer de-

cides what shall be seen and heard, but the reader seems
to be getting his material at firsthand, seems to be left to
draw his own conclusions without author's intervention.

Even when no stories result, attempts at objective treatment are good practice. They compel attention to be given
to externals, prevent fuzziness in recording those externals.
That man who last week turned away from the ticket window
in a rage—how did you know he was in a rage? What showed
it to you, standing two places in the line behind him? The
meek "yes" you heard some wife give back to her husband—
since you could not get inside her mind, how did you yet
know, as surely as though you had been inside, that the "yes"
meant "no"? How, still outside her mind, should you pass on
that knowledge to a reader?

At the extreme other end of the scale from the story told
objectively is the stream-of-consciousness story.

All the way home it grew worse. Eyes following her, eyes casting scorn on her. That big man over there on the park bench—he
hadn't looked but he had laughed, he and the boy beside him.
Because he had seen her reflection in the pond, of course. Seen
her hat upside down and under it her face. . . . But she could
have borne all that. It was Mrs. MacFarlane she couldn't bear.
Stopping her, holding out her hand, saying those things people
did say—"so glad . . . such a nice day . . . never saw you looking so well"—and her own voice answering, and all the while Mrs.
MacFarlane looking at the pavement, looking at the houses along
the street, never really seeing her at all, but something in her
smile, something sly, mocking, something that said, "I know about
it. I know you tried for that job and couldn't get it." She freed
her hand from Mrs. MacFarlane's—"*so* glad . . . yes—yes, of
course, I'll come . . . so busy—" She was off down the street.
But Mrs. MacFarlane's eyes were on her still. Smiling, smiling

above those fat cheeks, they measured her—"tried for a job and couldn't get it, couldn't get it, couldn't get it." She slammed her door behind her and ran to the curtained window to look out. Mrs. MacFarlane was coming slowly down the street, stopped to speak to some one. Smiling, smiling Mrs. MacFarlane, rejoicing all the while to think that she, Amy Selfridge—

Mrs. MacFarlane, of course, does not see herself in this fashion. Probably no one else sees her so; no one is spying or mocking, or even aware of the heroine's momentary tragedy. Another mind would make from the same materials something unrecognizably different. *Stream of consciousness,* then, is a name well chosen, for the effect it has on events in a story is singularly like the effect of moving water on the objects submerged in it. The pebbles in the bed of a brook show through the water, but they show with wavering outlines and altered colors.

It is characteristic of the stream-of-consciousness story that the author's examination of his character is always microscopic, with both the advantages and the defects of microscopy. The examination shows only a little, one mood, one trait, but it shows that little enormously magnified, made to fill the whole slide. What happens to the individual shown in relation to other surroundings, other moods, is pushed into the background. The one chosen mood is given prime consideration. Of all the points of observation, this one reduces farthest the value of externals, treating them as mood-causers and nothing else. Thus far, the stream-of-consciousness story has been most frequently used for the presentation of trivial or selfish beings or for recording the reactions of neurotics. The heroic emotions do not readily lend themselves to this treatment, perhaps because any character, examined microscopically, appears neurotic; perhaps because strength of character expresses itself in controlling events instead of merely sensing them.

Omniscience, on the other hand, allows for an observation of the mind as complete as that in the stream-of-consciousness story but allows for it from the outside. The author photographs minds; he does not enclose himself in them. And, as with all photographs, background appears as well as main figure. From his point of vantage, he finds and pictures relations, qualities, of which the individuals concerned know nothing.

O'Mallen was the product of a hate. Hate had created and moulded him, and it had done its work well.

Up to the time the hate entered his life, he had been merely the handsomest and most turbulent member of a turbulent and reckless family. Drinking and brawling, a month of labor with a week of tippling to follow—these were the family habits handed down from father to son. When, at the end of a breathless secret courtship, he had eloped with the only daughter of a neighbor and later been forgiven and gone to live with his wife's mother—

This is not O'Mallen as O'Mallen knows himself nor yet as his neighbors know him. It is the knowledge of a maker, looking down clear-sightedly on what has been made and naming the tool used in the making.

In *One Crowded Hour*, Ben Ames Williams explains of his hero, a farmer now in his fifty-seventh year, ". . . he had never had an adventure, had never suffered a catastrophe . . . married the daughter of a man whose farm lay on the other side. . . . He had never had any passion for her, though he had always liked her well enough—." Here, again, the author sees what no favorable placing of eye or ear, no following of his hero's thoughts could give him. About that hero, he relates what only a personal God could know and what none but an unscrupulous God would reveal. All the perquisites of a creator are his, along with all the difficulties. In the opening paragraphs of a story and in explanatory summaries, omniscience is a useful tool. For the length of a story, it is usually unwieldy. Rasselas, as readers will remember, "desired a little kingdom in which he might —— see all the parts of government with his own eyes." A writer, having drifted about from mind to mind, from conscious to subconscious, in the drafts of early stories, is likely to discover that he too is more content in a little kingdom. The kingdom most writers have chosen has been that of the external world with retreat at will into one mind but only one.

The wind had triumphed and swept all the clouds from heaven . . . Villon cursed his fortune. Would it were still snowing! Now, wherever he went he must weave, with his own plodding feet, the rope that bound him to the crime and would bind him to the gallows . . .

Two things preoccupied him as he went: the aspect of the gallows at Montfaucon in this bright, windy phase of the night's existence, for one; and for another, the look of the dead man with his bald head and garland of red curls. Both struck cold upon his heart, and he kept quickening his pace as if he could escape from unpleasant thoughts by mere fleetness of foot. Sometimes he looked back over his shoulder with a sudden nervous jerk; but he was the only moving thing in the white streets . . .

The excerpt is, of course, from Stevenson's *A Lodging for the Night*. Here the author keeps the story in his own hands, observing from some invisible vantage point what is to be seen and heard, drawing deductions from it, moving in and out of the minds of his persons but letting the subconscious alone, knowing of those minds only what their possessors also know.

Before exploring the question of which point of observation and which adaptation of that point a beginner may most hopefully try in his own story, one other question should receive at least a partial answer. The question is this: A point of observation having been established, how readily may it be changed? What does change cost?

Obviously, an "I" story cannot turn into a third-person one without multiple readjustments. Obviously, too, a stream-of-consciousness story cannot be altered to subordinate mood to events. Apart from these attempts to add apples and pears, the matter of shifts is chiefly a matter of economy. Ordinarily, a shift costs something in words used and costs still more in the demand it makes on the reader to readjust his mind. The writer looking over his story and finding the point of observation shifted several times has need to consider both these costs. If the shifts are meant to produce contrasts, to balance one personality against another, they may be worth while. If they are means only of getting information to the reader, then almost certainly they are sources of weakness and producers of a scrappy, disjointed narrative. In the excerpt from an amateur story which follows, it is evident that the movement from one person's mind to another's is not the result of a wish on the writer's part to display the working of two minds but only of his uncertainty as to how to keep his narrative moving.

Sir Henry hummed softly and blithely as he shaved. He was happy today, for his wife was to spend the week in the country.

He was glad to have a respite from her incessant nagging. . . . It had been this nagging and lack of understanding, in fact, that had made Helen come to be so attractive. It was not a clandestine affair or anything like that, of course, but he realized that his wife would never have understood. He had never told her of their intimacy.

It was a shame that a man could not be appreciated at home. It seemed mean and sordid to have to meet Helen and take her to places where they wouldn't meet any of their friends. Then he had to return and make excuses to his wife. Now, however, he would be free for a week. It would be pleasant to have Helen to dinner here in the apartment; he'd telephone her when he went out. He put away the dark suit he had worn the day before and got out a light, spring suit. As he stood at the mirror knotting his tie, there entered a very intelligent looking young man.

"Hello, Austin." Austin was not only the best laboratory assistant Sir Henry had ever had, but he had got him out of some tight places. For instance, that time when his wife had asked him who had been at dinner at the club.

"I beg your pardon, sir. I thought you would be ready to begin work." Then he noticed that Sir Henry had taken longer than usual to dress that morning, but he refrained from smiling. That was one of his accomplishments, he knew when not to smile.

"That's all right, Austin. I'm going down to Hurdon and Baker's this morning to see how that precipitation apparatus is working. Oh, and that American spiritualist is coming to see if I'll have a seance. I don't see why I should be pestered just because I once wrote an article on spiritualism for a review. We shall have to get rid of her.". . .

That afternoon time began to drag. He grew restless. He wondered when Helen would come. At last the doorbell rang.

"If it is the spiritualist, show her in here. If it is Helen, show her into the drawing-room."

He adjusted his necktie and walked through the portieres into the drawing-room. As he did so, Helen entered. . . . The bell rang again, and they heard Austin ushering the medium into the laboratory. They glanced at the thick portieres. They were tightly closed, and Sir Henry took Helen in his arms.

But they did not hear the door open a second time. They were too deeply interested in each other . . . But the door had opened again, and Austin emerged from the laboratory to see Lady Anne going through the door into the drawing-room. He rushed in at her heels, thinking faster than he had ever thought before. Here was a real problem for his genius as a diplomat. Austin stopped behind Lady Anne, frantically attracting Sir Henry's attention to a notebook. . . .

No gain in ease for the writer is likely to compensate for the dislocation of reader's interest caused by the two shifts, especially the latter one which places Austin suddenly in the main role. When a writer finds himself slipping from one point of observation to another, he is likely to find, on examination, that his decision as to what the story is he wants to write is equally unsteady. In general—though no "in general" can apply to every writer—a beginner should try other expedients before deciding on the use of several points of observation within a story. Practice with various points of observation, like practice with various time schemes, provides a profitable field for experiment. Some of those experiments are best performed on the work of other people. In the beginning paragraphs of Katherine Mansfield's *A Cup of Tea*, for example, would the heroine be less detestable if the story were told in the first person? Or would she be more detestable? Could it be so told? And if not all the way, how far? What would happen to the story if the point of observation were within the husband's mind?

Other paragraphs can be made to furnish answers for the same questions, but when a writer's own work is in question, what it usually requires first is not an examination of shifts within the story but an interrogation of the general point of observation. Some material shows at once that it can be told in one way only. But most stories, if they can be written at all, can be written with reasonable success from any of several standpoints. And yet only one of these several will bring out the full worth of the material to be used.

To gather all the important matter of a story into mind; to consider it as told in the first person, the main figure serving as "I"; as told in the third person, with entrance into the mind of the one character against whom the teller holds a grudge; as told omnisciently; as told by a teller reporting only what he sees through the wavering stream of one person's consciousness—this is a laborious process, but it is one which makes the worker at home with his narrative. After the point of observation for the whole work is decided beyond change, after the first draft is on paper, the time comes for considering shifts. Of each, one question should be asked in advance of any other, "Have I made this shift because nothing else will bring the effect I want, or have I made it to escape from mental effort?"

VI

Implication

"It's not so much the words you say
As the way in which you say them;
It's not so much the thoughts you convey
As the manner in which you convey them."
                    Nursery rhyme.

Suggested Reading

SALINGER, J. D. "Down at the Dinghy," in *Nine Stories*. Boston: Little, Brown.

MANSFIELD, KATHERINE. "Bliss," in *Bliss*. New York: Alfred A. Knopf.

GARRETT, GEORGE. "More Geese Than Swans Now Live." *The Sewanee Review*. Spring 1962.

STEGNER, WALLACE. "The Berry Patch," in *The Women on the Wall*. New York: The Viking Press, Compass Books.

"SAKI" (H. H. Munro). "The Open Window," in *The Short Stories of Saki*. New York: The Viking Press.

STEELE, WILBUR DANIEL. "Blue Murder," in *The Man Who Saw Through Heaven and Other Stories*. New York: Harper and Row.

FAULKNER, WILLIAM. "Mule in the Yard," in *Collected Stories of William Faulkner*. New York: Random House.

Implication

IMPLICATIONS in a story are exactly what their name denotes. They are statements presented not for themselves, or at least not chiefly for themselves, but for conveying to the reader something beyond the thing they say. An implication, that is, is a signpost. The signpost itself may or may not have value; the legend it bears must have. A signpost, however, may be set in any of three ways—with the legend facing the reader and thus immediately intelligible; with the blank side facing the reader, so that only after it is passed is its meaning perceived; with the legend visible, yet so worded as to be temporarily misleading. The legend can never be actually false; some suppression, some juggling with words, must always point a way out to truth.

A set of implications meant to be immediately plain—signposts with their legends facing towards the reader—is found in *Arrival,* by Mary Porter Russell.* The story, told in the third person from a child's point of observation, covers the arrival, and perhaps an hour of time after the arrival, of a mother and child at the mountain resort where the child's father is staying.

In that hour, husband and wife meet, stroll from the stage station to the husband's cottage, go to the spring for water, stroll back towards the house. The little girl's mental picturing of her father, while she is still on the stage, has told us

* In *Story,* May, 1937. Used by permission of The Editors.

directly that he has been ill. In the conversation between husband and wife, we learn, also directly, that he expects his family to stay only a month, that his wife purposes to stay until all three can leave together. These things are specifically told, are part of that bundle of information and immediate action which form the outer shell of any story. Accompanying them are two sets of implications by means of which the reader learns what the real story is—things never said but abundantly made clear.

> . . . father was helping them out of the car. . . . He looked terribly glad to see them, but when Joan tried to kiss him he turned his face to one side, so that she kissed only his cheek . . .
>
> Joan wanted water, but she couldn't find a glass. "There aren't any," said father. "I had two, but I broke them." She picked up a cup then, but he called out very quickly, "Here, don't take that. Don't ever use any of the dishes with pink flowers on them."
>
> "Why?" Joan asked him.
>
> "Because they are *my* dishes," said father. "I've always liked dishes with pink flowers, and at home your mother wouldn't let me have any. There are just enough for me. You two will have to get along with those with gold bands."

There are more of these signposts. What they say is what no one of them puts into words—that the father is tubercular, a danger therefore to his wife, doubly a danger to a young child.

These implications concern conditions already established in the lives of the three. Beside them runs another set dealing with things to come.

> "The little woman's as purty as a picture," said the driver, looking at mother. "Now I c'n see why yer wuz always hangin' around fer the mail."

Mother didn't look pleased, but father laughed. "Thank you, Jansen," he said. "Bring the bags around to the house later, will you? We're going to walk."

He took Joan's hand and mother's arm, and led them past the row of little stores, from which queer-looking people stood at the doors and stared. They wore rough old clothes, and the men needed to shave, and the women were very ugly. Father spoke to most of them and called their names.

"Jansen's a close friend of mine," he said. "Fine fellow."

Father turned in at the little house and opened the door. "Brookside Cottage welcomes you," he said.

There was a big stove inside and a lot of books and papers scattered around, and a lamp like people in the country used. It wasn't pretty at all, and back in the bedroom it was worse. There was no spread on the bed—just a red blanket on top, and it was all lumpy, as if the sheets underneath weren't smooth. Father's big, old slippers stuck out from under it.

Mother looked around and smiled. "Stand it for three months, honey?" asked father, who was watching her.

Here also the signs are turned towards the reader. He need be neither prophet nor son of prophet to let his mind run outside the boundaries of the story to the approaching disaster which it does not tell but foretells. By implication, though not by the presence of any printed word, the fate of the three is carried beyond the hour to which the writer limits himself. Kept within that hour imaginatively as it is chronologically, it would be too thin for any reader's interest.

Peacock in the Snow, by Benedict Thielen, is again a story in which the signposts bear legends immediately intelligible. The external action of the story is of the slightest. Two men, research workers at Harvard, go to call on a third who has married while on leave and has returned to Cambridge with his wife.

The story opens with presentation of its most important character—winter.

Snow was deep all the way out to the house . . . the air was cold and brisk . . . we all loved the cold sharp weather . . . the dry powdery snow would be good for skiing . . . the snow and the white-painted houses looked clean and cold. . . . Everything was black and white . . . the window on which the frost crystals glittered.

The phrases quoted are, of course, not consecutive. They are interrupted by factual dialogue, by the men's arrival at the house, by description of the exotic loveliness of the Southern wife. But snow outside, drafts under doors, a reluctant furnace—throughout the story these shout aloud to any reader the thing they never say. By means of them, Henry's happiness and his wife's beauty and brilliant talent are visibly, though never verbally, doomed.

In both the stories quoted so far, the implications cannot be mistaken. They are the writer's way of telling his story. He means them to be instantly understood. Illustrations of implications intentionally misleading are found in almost any of W. W. Jacobs' humorous stories. *A Question of Habit,* told by the night watchman on an anchored ship, begins with the sentence, "Wimmin aboard ship I don't 'old with," and runs through two paragraphs of critical comment on women's ways, leading to the admission, "O' course, sometimes you get a gal down the fo'c's'le pretendin' t' be a man. . . ." The story being told in the first person, a reader is fairly sure to take the teller's statements as though they were the author's. When a page or two later the skipper roars at the whimpering cabin boy, "Why, you ought to be at a young ladies' school," and the boy, whimpering the more, responds, "I know I ought, sir," readers are fully prepared to accept him for the girl he is not.

It has already been said that the statement from which a reader draws a false implication must not itself be false. In *A Question of Habit*, the teller never says, "Henry is a girl"; Henry himself is equally scrupulous. Having made his general comments about women, the watchman opens his illustrative story, "We 'ad a queer case once on a barque I was on," and a queer case it turns out to be. Literally taken, the assertion is accurate. So, too, when the startled skipper appeals to the cabin boy, "Don't tell me you're a girl!" the boy weepingly responds, "I won't if you don't want me to." A "yes" would throw the whole machinery of the narrative out of action. Newcomers to writing, justifying their expedients for getting a reluctant story forward, sometimes point out that, in the situation given, the person in the story would have lied. If the reader is to know the lie for a lie and know it instantly, then the person may; when the lie is recognizable, however, it is, of course, no help in establishing surprise.

Several paragraphs before the end of *A Question of Habit*, the hoax becomes apparent. The drawing out of the scene, seemingly to meet the needs of the skipper's slow comprehension, is really the reader's chance to relish his own almost as slow discovery. If, though, the reader chances to be a writer as well, he does not stop with relishing. He goes back over the story, observing what he may have missed at first reading. He finds that accompanying a full line of signposts which appear to read, "The cabin boy is a girl" is another line, unobtrusive but equally frequent, announcing, "He is a boy." Without this second set, the surprise at the end falls flat.

An unprepared-for surprise, that is, is one of the poorest of fictional properties. By means of it, anybody can escape from any propounded dilemma, but so much is left behind that the escape is not worth the making.

I heard his riotous retreat down the stairway. He was singing as he went and striking about with his umbrella. The crash of glass accompanied his progress and the shrieking of the other lodgers. Later we learned that he had long been confined in an asylum.

In 1872, the date of the story from which the excerpt above is taken, that unheralded "later we learned" could evidently pass muster, at least to the extent of getting itself printed. It cannot now. Unless within the story itself there are unobtrusive evidences of madness—enough of them so that the "he was mad" is actually a superfluous ending— then the story, according to the standard of even the least demanding of today's reading groups, is botched work, with no chance of acceptance.

Thus far, the implications treated have been those important to the action of the story. Frequently they pertain instead to character, to economic or social placing, to the relation between persons. Witness the opening of Alice Duer Miller's *Plum Pudding and Mince Pie*.

In a small New England village it was being said that the four Warren boys were coming home for Christmas. . . . That is to say, an English servant had put two pigskin bags in a compartment on a fast train east from Chicago. A gentleman in evening dress had left a great public dinner after the speech of the evening, his own, in order to catch the midnight to Boston. A staff car had driven to the Union Station in Washington and had there deposited a colonel in the United States Army so that he might get a train to Boston without changing at New York. A cruiser that had seen service in the war had come to anchor in Hampton Roads just in time for the commanding officer to catch this same train.

The facts are given in concise statement; it is their implication, not the facts themselves, which makes the paragraph important.

A reader's getting a bad start with a story, believing it to be about one thing and finding on the third page that he must reorient himself, comes usually from implications introduced too late.

Rick Davis, whom Pap Johnson called, without affection, "the village brat," paused on the rocky ledge and pointed out various familiar landmarks in the valley to Rita, Pap's blue-eyed daughter. The entrance to the unheralded McCoy Caverns was at their backs, a jagged hole in the side of the rugged little mountain which formed part of Virginia's Blue Ridge.

Probably the very inaccessibility of the entrance had preserved these caves from the fate of their sisters to the north, and the much publicized Shenandoah and Luray Caverns. At any rate no one paid exorbitant prices to view the superior splendors of the McCoy; in fact, if any one was hardy enough to climb the mountain, over boulders and through brambles, just to slide down into the maw of the earth, he had certainly paid enough of a price to entitle him to look his fill. Few of the inhabitants of the little mountain community in the valley had ever seen the treasures of nature in those caverns. Rick was one of the few, Rita was not.

The mere thought of this day-long expedition with red-headed

Rick, who had won her heart with guitar and voice, had been enough to elevate Rita to the fleece-lined heavens known only to those who truly love. And there was no doubt but that she loved this lanky, lazy mountaineer. Hadn't she thrown herself into his strong arms and wept for joy on his bony shoulder when he asked for her hand the other night? And hadn't she defended him from ridicule? Hadn't she prayed to God for his salvation? Of course she loved him.

With a negligent arm thrown across the shoulders of his bride-to-be, Rick continued to gesture across the valley with his free hand . . .

In these four opening paragraphs, the story has seemed to be that of a lovers' expedition, with suggestion of parental opposition, of possible danger from the descent into the cavern. When, later, the reader discovers that Rick has planned to murder his Rita inside the cave, that "later" is quite too late. The inaccessibility of the cavern does indeed suggest danger but not that danger, any more than Rita's attitude towards Rick suggests his having already seduced her. Direct statement is, of course, impossible. The opening sentences cannot say, "Rick means to murder Rita" nor yet, "Rita is to have a child." What they can do is to establish in the reader's mind an attitude towards Rick in accord with what he intends presently to attempt. The properties now attributed to him—"red-headed". . . "with guitar and voice". . . "lanky". . . "lazy"—carry no condemnation. The father's epithet is discounted because it is the father who utters it, and every reader is aware of how fictional fathers feel towards the lovers of fictional daughters. Readers begin to make up their minds as soon as they begin to read. They cannot avoid doing so. It is when he begins to read, therefore—not on the second page, not on the third—that a reader must be guided towards the main attitudes the writer wants him to have.

Late implication, such as in the example just given, comes from lack of practice in writing. The opening point in time having been chosen, there is so much to be said that the writer cannot pick out which are the matters finally important. Wrong implication, on the other hand, when it is not meant to produce a later surprise, comes usually from a writer's changing his mind as the story proceeds—comes, along with a host of other shortcomings, from the author's not having given the story enough thought before it was put on paper.

"Hurry up, Mary." He didn't know that this command irritated his wife a little more each time he repeated it. He didn't see her clench her teeth as she waited for the emphasis to fall, each time, on exactly the right part of "hurry." Nor, if he had seen, would he have paid attention. Florence was coming in on the Panama Pacific liner today. Let's see, yes, close to three and a half hours from now she'd be in. Well, of course, it was only one hour's drive to the dock, but they wanted to be sure and be there when Florence arrived. He'd been ready for at least two hours, and why in heaven's name Mary had to gather up the laundry at a time like this was more than he could understand.

"Ma—ry, hurry up."

"Tom! Florence's boat won't be in for three hours at least. You're not helping me by hurrying me like this. These things have got to be attended to before we leave, and I can get a lot more done if you will just keep out of my way for half an hour. You haven't read the newspaper yet. It's out in the kitchen, Tom. Go on and read it."

He drew himself from the chair and, without a word, left the room. Newspaper, hell! Might glance through it, though. The front page with its three-inch bold-face headlines . . . covered with words. He read the words and they stayed words. Couldn't get beyond words. Didn't mean anything.

"Mary," he called from the kitchen, "what car are we going in?"

"The sedan, of course."

"Let's drive Florence's car. She would be sort of pleased, don't you think?"

"And Florence's bags, Tom?"

"Oh, they'd fit in the rumble seat."

No sound from the bedroom . . . maybe she was at last ready.

"Mary, you're about ready, aren't you?"

"Tom!"

. . . they left two hours later in the sedan.

There is no lack of implication here. The father's eagerness for his daughter's return, the effect of that eagerness on his wife, the marital discipline he endures—all these are fully developed in the opening page. Two pages later, however, the domineering mother drops from view, the father becomes the tyrant over his daughter. The story promises one thing, then presents quite another. No matter how adequately the second thing is presented, there is still a break, a need for readjustment. Poe's much quoted dictum is not always a dependable guide, but as concerns the signposts set along a story's road, it is safe to follow. Each legend must say what will finally help out the story's purpose, its "preconceived effect." "If his very initial sentence tend not to the outbringing of this effect, then he has failed in his first step."

But while implications introduced too late spring from a writer's failing to realize for which important things his readers need to be prepared, and false implication from his having failed to think out his story, lack of implication arises usually from a mental attitude far more difficult to alter. It arises, that is, from the writer's certainty that what he has said is sufficient, that from it any reader should be able to do his own inferring. Sir Walter Scott's

> I do not write for that dull elf
> Who cannot picture for himself—

is the instinctive protest of every shallow writer, who enjoys the titillation of imagining but hates the drudgery of making his imaginings clear. There is instruction to be gained by hunting out the rest of Scott's passage and discovering the minute exactness with which he proceeds to tell his readers, dull and otherwise, precisely what it is they shall picture.

Thinness, squeezing out from a story all except its explicit statements, is the most difficult of all faults to remedy. Only after a considerable experience with first drafts is it possible to believe that it can be remedied, either in an individual story or in the later work of the same writer. Many times it cannot; for flat-mindedness, whether in writing or elsewhere, is a persistent characteristic. Sometimes, however, the flatness is on the page only, not actually in the mind. As a help to removing it, try going over some paragraphs or pages of a story you admire, considering what is said, what is made known without being said. Scott Fitzgerald's *The Jelly-Bean,* for example, speaks only ill of its hero for the length of its seventy-odd opening words. Which of the words put down, what words left out, show you that, against the author's assertion, the figure is to be likable? Katherine Mansfield, in *A Cup of Tea,* characterizes Rosemary Fell as "young, brilliant, extremely modern, exquisitely dressed, amazingly well read in the newest of the new books." By exactly what words is she already condemned in advance of the actually condemning phrases to follow?

When a beginner is very much a beginner, and sometimes even when he is not, it is useful to set down in parallel columns the information directly given and that given by implication in whatever passage is under consideration. It is useful too to pause at the end of the first page of somebody else's writing, summarize in mind the impressions gained, then search back for their sources. After you have considered somebody else's work, and after you have then turned back again to your own, do you find that you have too many explicit statements? too few? Besides what is told directly, phrases on which you can put your finger, what else will a reader have discovered? What are the phrases which, while they leave a certain thing unsaid, yet cause the reader to know that thing? If no phrase tells him, what omissions, what juxtapositions, do the telling?

VII

Characterization

. . . and if the world had been made of machinery, he would have had the fee simple of happiness.

But to both happiness and misery there follows the inevitable second act, and beyond that, and to infinity, action and interaction, involution and evolution, forging change forever. Thus he failed to take into consideration that the lady was alive . . .

—JAMES STEPHENS, *Here Are Ladies**

* By permission of The Macmillan Company, publishers

Suggested Reading

HALL, LAWRENCE SARGENT. "The Ledge." *Hudson Review,* Winter 1958-59.

STEINBECK, JOHN. "The Leader of the People," in *The Long Valley.* New York: The Viking Press, Compass Books.

USTINOV, PETER. "God and the State Railways." *The Atlantic,* August 1961.

BOWEN, ELIZABETH. "Ivy Gripped the Steps," in *Ivy Gripped the Steps.* New York: Alfred A. Knopf.

CHEKHOV, ANTON. "The Darling," in various short-story collections.

ROSTEN, LEO. "The Case for Mr. Parkhill," in *The Return of H*y*m*a*n K*a*p*l*a*n.* New York: Harper and Row.

WELTY, EUDORA. "A Worn Path," in *A Curtain of Green and Other Stories.* New York: Harcourt, Brace and World.

JAMES, HENRY. "The Real Thing," in *Novels and Tales of Henry James.* New York: Charles Scribner's Sons.

PORTER, KATHERINE ANNE. "Flowering Judas," in *Flowering Judas and Other Stories.* New York: Harcourt, Brace and World.

Characterization

I

THE word *character* has accumulated in English more uses than it can comfortably carry, and this both in speech or in writing. When we say, "Bertrand has a fine character," we are likely to be referring praisefully to an actual being. When we say, "Bertrand is a fine character," the chances are that Bertrand is a figure in a story or a play. When, removing the adjective, we say, "Bertrand certainly is a character," Bertrand may be either real or imagined, but in neither case is our pronouncement flattering to him.

In a story, the so-called minor characters—or even the major ones—may actually have been given no more character than billiard balls. When one of these characterless characters is distinguished from the rest, the writer has then "characterized" his character. If he is distinguished by absurdities, he has become "a character."

Within the length of this chapter, then, where much is to be said of character, of characteristics and characterization, the word *person* is used to denote that imagined individual about whom the writer writes. *Character* is that which the writer bestows upon the person by means of the characteristics assigned to him. He makes him "certainly a character" only when he makes him a caricature.

With this preliminary establishment of terminology, we

enter upon discussion of the most difficult and incommunicable of the skills involved in writing.

II

The ability to characterize is without doubt the most important single ability a fiction writer can possess, whether short story writer or novelist. Unfortunately it is also, above all others, the one which nobody can teach him. A chapter dealing with characterization, if it is to avoid sham, has to begin with that regrettable admission. The utmost such a chapter can offer are the five forms of aid listed below.

a) It can set down warnings against those faults in characterization peculiar to amateur writing.

b) It can note the differences between presentation in the round, presentation in profile, and caricature—differences worth a good deal of any writer's thought.

c) It can point out the kind of story in which characterization is important, the kinds in which its importance is diminished or absent.

d) It can discuss the relation between the persons and the happenings in a story.

e) It can suggest devices (they are no more than that) for keeping the mind inquisitive about human attitudes.

First, then, for the warnings: Except in the rarest cases, a short story writer should not attempt to delineate character by setting down multiplied details of personal appearance. Any writer, stopping at the nearest post-office and reading the descriptions of escaped criminals posted there, can prove this point for himself. In fiction, description is always a form of characterization; it has no other use. Either the outside look of the person is to correspond with his character and thus reveal it, or it is to differ from his character and thus produce a temporary deception. But whether for revelation or deception, no author can compel a reader to carry in mind a dozen differing details. Even when other drawbacks are disregarded, the one heavy drawback of the reader's having to alter and re-alter his conception of the imaginary person is alone enough to discourage detailed description. Equally discouraging is the waste of space involved.

Alida was fair and small and pretty, with blue eyes and yellow hair. Her skin was delicately pink and white. Her little, firm-set, red mouth, and her thin, straight nose were as small as the features of a child. Her chin was tiny too, but her eyes and forehead were as much too large for her face as her nose and mouth were small. In the plain little blue or brown or white dresses which she most affected, she looked not unlike a child. Her quick, determined walk, though, and her voice, deeper than that of most women, showed all the maturity with which twenty-four years had invested her.

The passage is not badly worded. The description does not, as amateur attempts often do, stop short with outer appearance; by means of outer appearance, it does give glimpses of character. But for those glimpses, there are used a hundred and eleven words. A third of these can be deleted without loss. Two thirds can go with only slight rearrangement. In a novel, such lavish presentation is occasionally serviceable. In a short story, it is unlikely to be. The word limits which hedge about even the longest story make sure of that. Wodehouse explains of one of his persons,

She had bright bulging eyes and a lot of yellow hair, and when
she spoke she showed about fifty-seven front teeth,

and so is done with her, with character in plenty set in
front of the reader's eyes.

Minnie, age eleven, brown-skinned, square-templed, placid . . .

is all the personal description Minnie, age eleven, is likely
to need, though in her original presentation in an amateur's
story, twenty-two additional words diluted the ones here
given.

O. Henry's well-known hero "looked amiable and freck-
led" and no more, and yet no reader would be likely to complain of his being under-characterized. Edith Wharton's
famous "Mrs. Ballinger is one of those ladies who pursue
Culture in bands, as though it were dangerous to meet alone"
certainly calls for no additions. Edith Wharton, indeed, is
perhaps especially well worth watching for the thrifty brev-
ity with which she introduces her people, usually giving personal description only the smallest place, if any, in her
presentations.

For characterization, then, a particular feature, a mannerism, a line of heaped adjectives present an impression
sharp and clear in the reader's mind, one that calls for no
remaking. Multiplied details lead ordinarily only to vague-
ness.

The earliest characterization of a figure is, of course, the
most important, the one that sets the tune for all the rest.
H. G. Wells, in *The Man Who Could Work Miracles,* puts
the miracle-working power into the hands of ". . . a little
man . . . eyes of a hot brown, very erect red hair, and a

moustache with ends that he twisted up, and freckles. His name was George McWirter Fotheringay . . . and he was a clerk at Gomshott's." There is no derogation, moral or intellectual, in any of the items noted, but Fotheringay is endowed with pettiness nonetheless. The pettiness is never stated, but it is there beyond any later rescue.

Except for some special reason, a writer should not offer by means of author's statement what is later to be proved or contradicted by his person's actions.

She was witty and charming to everybody.

Her popularity sprang from her gaiety, which made her the life of any party.

If a direct view of the person is to be given, if dialogue is to be included, the author's attributions make it only that much the harder to convince a reader who has been warned to expect much. And on the writer's side, the habit of trusting to general assertion and thus sliding away from exact presentation is one no beginner can afford to form. A figure in a story is a little like an actor walking the stage. What can be told about him on the playbill is insignificant contrasted with what his own entrance, his slightest speech, can do.

This prohibition does not hold, of course, for stories told in the first person. In a first-person story, the "I" is entitled to his opinion. It does not hold, either, as concerns the recording of the effect of one character on another. "He found her witty and charming" requires no bolstering.

A writer is unwise to use the persons in his narrative, or any one of them, for ends unrelated to the story's original intent. Dorothy Canfield, in her comment on the genesis of *Flint and Fire,* speaks of putting in and later taking out of her story a person introduced only to vent annoyance against a visitor who had arrived while the story was in progress. Every writer has had similar experiences. Stories in plenty, and good stories, have been born out of irritation, but the irritations which occur after a story is already in progress have usually no honest place in it.

And even though a story owes its conception to irritation or to personal injury, it still requires special pondering and delay if it is not to be a waste of the writer's time. Stories by the thousand have had their inception in hurts which have disappeared by the time the third page is written. Even if the hurt continues unabated, it is still likely to pull the narrative out of its course, bend it towards the justifying of its injured creator. The author who caused his jilted heroine to thrust into her fiction a foiled and publicly disgraced adventuress "so like her rival that, at the last moment, she was terrified and added a few disfiguring moles" was exploiting an all but universal tendency. Personal annoyances, personal grievances need ordinarily to be revalued in terms other than the personal before they are ready for use. Impersonal emotional disturbances—generous indignations, pities, admirations—are the very yeast of fiction, but even with these, deliberation has its advantages. If, its first draft being completed, the story born of a sudden intense emotion were laid away for cooling, some few admirable things might be lost, but the saving of time now squandered on the working and re-working of the impossible would be enormous.

The prohibitions just set down are not absolute. There are exceptions to every one, just as there are exceptions to any statement, positive or negative, which can be made about writing. But the lapses here pointed out are those to which beginners are prone. Added together, the negatives come at last to an affirmative: The writer shall deal honestly with his human material. He deals with it in what terms he pleases—in terms of fantasy, idealization, mockery, exact representation—but each of his persons requires to be made of one piece, and this means that each must have become of a piece in his own mind. Time for scrutiny, for re-evaluation, for winding the mind about the subject, is needed at every stage of fiction writing, but most of all is it needed in the consideration of character. Of all the "Thou shalt not's," the inclusive one is "Thou shalt not begin without prior meditation."

Every writer, of course, founds his presentations on persons he has known. Inventing a person is like inventing an animal; all that invention can do is to combine differently what already exists. Rarely, however, are a writer's presentations photographs, unless composite ones. Stevenson, who habitually analyzed his own writing processes, says of the creation of John Silver:

And then I had an idea for John Silver from which I promised myself funds of entertainment: to take an admired friend of mine . . . to deprive him of all his finer qualities and higher graces of temperament, to leave him with nothing but his strength, his courage, his quickness, and his magnificent geniality, and to try to express these in terms of the culture of a raw tarpaulin. Such physical surgery is, I think, a common way of "making character"; perhaps it is, indeed, the only way. We can put in the quaint figure that spoke a hundred words with us yesterday by the wayside; but do we know him? Our friend, with his infinite variety and flexibility, we know—but can we put him in? Upon the first we must engraft secondary and imaginary qualities, possibly all wrong; from the second, knife in hand, we must cut away and deduct the needless arborescence of his nature; but the trunk and the few branches that remain we may at least be fairly sure of.

That "trunk and the few branches," freed of choking underbrush, is what the beginner strives for.

III

The suggestions given in the preceding section can be tested against the background of almost any story the writer happens to have read. Before their efficacy in regard to his own stories can be decided, however, two decisions must have been reached.

One of these decisions is whether the persons he is about to present, if they are to be characterized at all, are to be presented in the round, in profile, or by caricature. In terms borrowed from another art, is the writer attempting a statue, a bas-relief, a cartoon?

Nobody supposes a bas-relief to be the whole man, but it may suggest the man, emphasize his salient point, as effectively as does a fuller representation. It is sometimes even more effective, since it is necessarily greatly simplified. In the same fashion, presentation of a person through some one trait is often effective by reason of its single-minded directness of aim. Presentation of a trait, however, and the presentation which attempts the encompassing in words of a whole person are different acts—acts different in kind, not only in degree. They presuppose different approaches by the writer to his story, a different attitude towards the person he is presenting, a different purpose as regards his readers. If a beginner has not already thought out these differences, he would do well to pause a long time over each of the phrases just used.

For the differences involved are more than merely those which concern amount of selection. Selection goes on in both processes. The gulf between the two presentations is not that the writer takes this and rejects that in one instance or the other. The important difference lies in what he does, or tries to do, with the material remaining in his hands.

When his attempt is to encompass a person, his attention is centered on making his readers acquainted with that person. When he is presenting a single trait dressed out in human form, his attention is on making all his readers feel for that personified trait one particular and limited emotion. For illustration of this difference, let us look at two stories, *Paul's Case,* by Willa Cather, and *Good Wednesday,* by Katharine Brush.

Paul, a lad of high-school age, is, objectively viewed, a thoroughly bad lot. He is a torment at school, an anxiety at home, a persistent liar, a worshiper of false values, finally a thief and a suicide. His teachers unanimously dislike him, their dislike built up on the boy's glitteringly defiant manner, on the unconcealed contempt with which he meets them. Readers, however, even from the opening of the story, are less unanimous than are the teachers. Paul is disagreeable always, is repulsive always. But among ten individuals following his story, there may readily be ten different shades of feeling towards him. Pity may predominate, or sympathy, or sheer distaste. The weight of his shortcomings may rest, in the reader's mind, on Paul himself, on his neighborhood, on society at large, even on Destiny. The same unhappy lad, the same appearance, actions, gestures, speeches are placed before all; the reactions are widely different.

Willa Cather, that is, is engaged in presenting a human being. Paul is shown in the round. So is Ethan in *Ethan Frome*. So—and with an amazing economy—are Major and Mrs. Monarch in Henry James' *The Real Thing*.

This is not to say that in any one of these stories there does not exist a common denominator in the feelings of readers towards the persons characterized. Such a common denominator is always present. But it is that and no more. Enough is shown to enable a reader to make his individual evaluation—one made in the terms of his own experience and what his temperament has made of that experience. Within the boundaries of one family, the father may carry Mulvaney warm in his heart, the mother relegate *Soldiers Three* to a high shelf to prevent the children from meeting him, and the young son, having found him there, push the book back into place, voting Mulvaney a bore.

When what is presented is not a character but an embodied trait, these differences of feeling do not exist. The writer has decided in advance how all readers shall feel; he presents only what must make them feel so. In *Good Wednesday,* a middle-aged hairdresser is depicted as she appears from the time she gets up in the morning till she starts for prayer meeting at night. Throughout the day, she goes from client to client in the small town where she practices. With each client, she leaves some morsel of malicious gossip, some virulently harmful deduction or invention. From each, she takes away a bit to be enlarged and embroidered for later use. Liking for her on any reader's part is out of the question. So is pity. So is the shifting from her of responsibility for her acts

—a shifting unconsciously performed by many readers of *Paul's Case*. Presumably, with the hairdresser quite as much as with Paul, there are reasons why she is as she is; presumably there may be moments when she is otherwise. But no hint of such moments or such causes enters the story. It is not a person, it is a trait, and that of petty malignity, which moves convincingly through the pages.

A second difference between presentation of character and that of trait is that presentation of character involves usually no moral judgment on the part of either writer or reader. Witness Mulvaney in *The Courting of Dinah Shadd*. Witness Rip Van Winkle. Even the horrid beings who inhabit Katharine Fullerton Gerould's *Wine of Violence* are not beings open to inevitable condemnation. The reader shudders at them, but the causes for their actions, the impulsions which left them helpless in the hold of hates stronger than they, speak up in their behalf, even as against a performance itself outside the range of human sympathy.

Successful presentation of a trait, on the other hand, involves on the author's part not only determination of exactly how readers shall feel but also determination to make that feeling righteous as well as unanimous. The author's selection from his person's actions has therefore to be limited even more strictly than the trait itself demands. Consistency is his first requirement. Everything—act, speech, gesture, thoughts —must enforce not only the trait to be shown but also the reader's detestation or admiration of that trait. For presentation of character, on the other hand, selection, though it has always to be made, yet has a wide range. No story can compass a man. But the base on which the writer builds is narrow in the one instance, broad in the other.

For caricature, the base is much the same as for presentation of a trait. Selection is equally narrow, but the trait presented is so enhanced as to be implausible except within the special atmosphere provided by the story. Miss Baxter, in *Good Wednesday,* can be transferred out of her story. "So-and-so is like that," is one of the most usual of readers' reactions. There is more difficulty in transferring Gash Tuttle, hero of Irvin Cobb's *Smart Aleck,* from page to life. There is still more in transferring Bertie Wooster, Wodehouse's many-times-used hero. Inside the story he can produce the momentary credulity needed for enjoyment, but no admirer places him in an actual scene, compares him with a living being. A caricature demands not only selection as rigid as that required for a personified trait, but also a surrounding and magnifying atmosphere outside of which the figure cannot live.

Which, then, have you meant to present in your story? Which have you presented?

As between caricature on the one hand and either character or personified trait on the other, distinction is not difficult. Unless he be extremely inexpert, the writer who is drawing a caricature knows he is doing so. He knows his figure will have reality to the reader only inside the setting, the thickened or rarefied air, he has intentionally created for him. If, in your own instance, however, you have doubts— if, that is, you think you have shown character but, at uneasy later reading, suspect an unintended caricature—the first and easiest of tests is the transference just suggested. In your own mind, can the imaginary figure be set down in everyday surroundings? Can he walk up your front steps, carry on his recorded conversation in your living room, and not be adjudged insane by any listener? To such readers as have met him, Mr. Quilp is probably as fully alive as Becky Sharp, but, unlike Becky, he cannot be made to travel. His uncanny river-edge residence, his saucepan of boiling gin, the dog in the lane which "lives on the left side but usually lurks on the right," are essential to his existence. He is a special figure, made for special purpose, allegorical as all caricatures are, and not at any moment to be taken for actual.

If, then, there is a possibility that the figure you have made has, against your purpose, grown disproportionate, one over-swollen feature concealing all the rest, make the disproportion obvious to yourself by change of environment. Whether, having been made obvious, it can be altered is far from sure. Caricatures, once created, have a dismal habit of staying so, and a story containing as its main figure an unintended caricature is usually better abandoned than tinkered with. Ordinarily, the most you can hope to gain from experiments at improvement is knowledge of what not to do another time.

Instances in which, meaning to present a character, you have instead feebly presented a personified trait, are less easy to discover. In the first draft of a story, there is no reason for your pausing to consider which you are committing to paper. As nearly as you can, you put down in that first draft whatever it is you want to say about your persons. But reading the draft over after it has cooled, or reading it aloud to a listener not committed in advance to approval, you find that what has reached the page is very far from being what you directed towards it. Whether trait or character, your main figure is ill-defined, incredible to the listener, uninteresting to him. The emotion he arouses is wavering or is too faint even to waver.

Changing the main figure to new surroundings, visualizing him inside your house or office gives little help. Those are transitions which can be accomplished by a person, by a personified trait, by a nonentity. What is most likely to be useful is an examination, as honest as you can make it, of your feelings towards your own creation. If it is a feeling all of one texture—all hate, all scorn, all mockery, all unqualified admiration; if you expect readers to feel as you do, would consider your story a failure if they felt otherwise, then probably what you are presenting is an isolated trait. The feebleness of the presentation may spring from your having allowed yourself too broad a base of observation. Try the story over, action after action, speech after speech. Does any speech or action fail to give some push towards the desired end? Does any action, any speech, push unintentionally in an opposite direction? Reread *Good Wednesday,* watching the sureness with which the writer thrusts her victim towards complete denunciation. If you are presenting a trait, if you are drawing a figure about which all readers are to feel in one way and only one, then you can afford no divergences. There your trait must stand, undiminished by conflicting traits.

There is, however, a second and a more serious reason for the failure of amateur stories setting forth a personified trait. If you are placing a trait on paper, are you sure beyond all question that the trait itself—not your presentation of it but the raw trait—appears to other eyes as it does to yours? Being sure of that, are you sure too that the placing given your person does not too far mitigate either his shortcoming or his virtue? Will the embodiment of fault-finding you have created seem to one reader mildly pathetic by reason of his age, to another justified because of enforced loneliness, and to both dull because their minds have failed to jump with yours?

Unaided, a writer rarely unearths in his own mind either of these possibilities. The trait, good or bad, which he is presenting seems to him unchangeably so. Since good is good and detestability is detestability, why should readers have differences of opinion about them?

A widened worldly experience is the best help here, but experience is slow to come by. If you have the habit of rigid classification, and still more if you entertain the set conviction that you do not have the habit, two steps towards improvement are open to you. One of these, of course, is an examination of how people around you, but outside your immediate family or group, feel towards characteristics which to you are faultless or irretrievably black. This examination, however, is valuable only after a suspicion has arisen in your mind that differences on the point in question are possible. An oblique fashion of discovering that they are is a return to the past. *'Tis All For the Best,* by Hannah More, displays a reduced gentlewoman whose repeated expression of meek trust is embodied in the title of the story.

Though Mrs. Simpson was the daughter of a clergyman and the widow of a genteel tradesman, she had been reduced, by a series of misfortunes, to accept a room in an almshouse. . . . One fine evening, as she was sitting reading her Bible . . . who should come and sit down by her but Mrs. Betty, who had formerly been lady's maid at the nobleman's house in the village of which Mrs. Simpson's father had been minister.

. . . But when Mrs. Simpson kindly addressed her as an old acquaintance, she screamed with surprise, "What you, madam? You in an almshouse, living on charity; you who used to be so charitable yourself . . ." "That may be one reason, Betty," re-

plied Mrs. Simpson, "why Providence has provided this refuge for
my old age. And my heart overflows with gratitude when I look
back on His goodness." "No such great goodness," said Betty.
"Why, you were born and bred a lady, and are now reduced to
live in an almshouse." "Betty, I was born and bred a sinner, un-
deserving of the mercies I have received." "No such great mercies," said Betty. "Why, I heard that you had been turned out of
doors; that your husband had broke; and that you had been in
danger of starving.". . . "It is all true, Betty; glory be to God,
it is all true." "Well," said Betty, "you are an odd sort of gentlewoman."

There is no question that Mrs. More admires her principal
figure, presents her for admiration. Do you admire her? If
not, why not? How do you feel toward the main figures in
Miss Edgeworth's *Waste Not, Want Not?* Toward the heroine of Washington Irving's *The Pride of the Village?* A careful look at the presentation of traits once all white, once all
black, but now by no means so unspeckled, wakes the mind
to meditation on its own certitudes. These, critically in-
spected, may turn out to be those of a single clique, a single
household, a particular segment of country, their power over
others no greater than that of the Widow Simpson over you.
Turning your mind around, if it is flexible enough to be
turned, try looking at your presented trait from the other
side. If you were not convinced in advance of its rightness
or wrongness, how would the person presented look to you
then? Is there a chance that its consistency in good or in
evil is a consistency implausible to every one but you? In the
twentieth century, what are the traits inevitably to be admired, inevitably to be despised? Or are there any?

These, of course, are long-range questions. For the story
immediately in hand, once your suspicion has been aroused

about it, all you can do is to let it lie by long enough after finishing to be sure that your judgment is less partial than in the course of writing; then subject it to inquiry as critical as you know how to make it. If you are part of a group, writing under guidance, differences of opinion within the group may help to dissolve your doubts, but in the last analysis you have to be your own critic. Your private critics—the relative or the friend or the pair of friends to whom you offer a reading of your work—are fairly sure to have, in the main, your own limitations or to be too tender of them to venture on criticism other than favorable.

Counsel given thus far is for avoiding or strengthening a caricature or a single-trait presentation. If what you are striving to put into words is a human being, full-size and in the round, then whatever this book can do for you is found in chapters other than this one. The time required for your person's presentation can be considered, the point of observation favorable to displaying him, the phrases for his characterization. But to capture understanding of the person himself is your own intimate struggle. Help there can be general only, not specific.

IV

At the opening of the section just finished, it was noted that two decisions about the persons to be presented in a story must be reached by a writer before his attention is turned to means of presentation. The second of these decisions relates not to how a writer is to characterize his figures but to whether it is necessary for him to characterize them at all. Are statue, bas-relief, caricature, any of them, called for in the story he has in hand? Or is the function of the figure to be that of the peg on a cribbage board—something the player moves to show that the game has progressed?

Not all stories call for characterization. Not even all important and lasting stories do. *The Arabian Nights* stands up fairly well against the assaults of time, and the caliph in one of those delectable tales is as like the caliph in another as toothpick is like toothpick. Nor is the lack of characterization limited to caliphs. A *Sindbad the Sailor* altered by the introduction of an individualized or an emotion-stirring Sindbad would be a *Sindbad the Sailor* ruined. In Wilkie Collins' *Story of a Terribly Strange Bed*, the hero's love of excitement leads him into gambling. To this extent, characterization gives aid to plot, for it is his gambling which brings money into his possession. If, however, the person concerned had been a priest carrying his congregation's offering to the Bishop; an heiress, young or old, with part of her patrimony on her person, the central events of the story would have moved exactly as they do now, unaltered by alteration of the main figure's rightness or wrongness, age or sex or occupation. What is important is only the known presence of money, not who carries it.

Characterization, then, is not, like repetition, a matter to be dealt with in every story. The story which presents a puzzle for the reader's solving, the one devoted to presentation of an inevitable emotion, the allegory, the trick story— with each of these the total effect may well be reduced, not heightened, by the bringing alive of any of the figures concerned. Why, in a detective story, is the reader willing to have the figures in the story knocked over like tenpins, a new one dead on the doorstep every time the door opens?

The reason is that they are tenpins; the writer has made them so. Enjoyment is decreased or destroyed if they are advanced to any more animated state. Detective stories containing careful characterization do exist, but the lasting ones, the exemplars, have little of it. So far as the detective himself is concerned, whether Dupin or Sherlock Holmes, he displays himself only as a collection of identifying mannerisms. The same mannerisms—of nonchalance, of reticence, of sudden revelation—serve for both, as they serve also for their important successors. Hercule Poirot is given a spice of vanity, a non-English syntax; Charlie Chan, a set of Orientalisms in speech and manner, but these too are properties rather than characterizations. As for the beings the detectives bring to justice or the beings they save from destruction, it is a fairly recent reader who can distinguish one from another unless by means of physical mark or setting. Where sequence of happenings is of prime importance, exactitudes of characterization make an unjustified demand on attention. In the original, not the derived, sense of the word, they are impertinent.

They are impertinent too in a story dealing with emotions so simplified as to be universal. In Poe's *Descent into a Maelstrom,* the "I" who tells of the descent has white hair, has been a fisherman, is now broken. This much the reader is told, but this goes no farther in characterization than would the man's having been a grocery clerk, retired because of rheumatism. The figure shown is representative only. It is humanity itself, not some identified particle from the mass, which makes that unparalleled descent. In the greater number of *Tales of Horror,* the same thing is true of the "I" who acts as teller. It is true of the "I" or the "he" in thousands of ghost stories. The conditions set forth in them are conditions by which every human being would be affected as is the hero; there is no point, then, in distinguishing him from others.

There is no point either in distinguishing the figures in an allegory. Mr. Worldly Wiseman is worldly wise—no more. He is a "character" only in the special sense of the word. To find this kind of "Character" in its perfection and to find too from what the personified trait draws its being, a reader can do no better than to turn back to collections put together in the seventeenth century, when the "Seventeenth-Century Character" was plentiful enough to gain a special designation.

1. The Obstinate Man does not hold opinions, but they hold him; for when he is once possest with an error, 'tis like the Devil, not to be cast out but with great difficulty. Whatsoever he lays hold on, like a drowning man, he never loses though it do but help to sink him the sooner. . . . The slighter and more inconsistent his Opinions are, the faster he holds them, otherwise they would fall asunder of themselves; for opinions that are false ought to be held with more Strictness and Assurance than those that are true, or they will betray their Owners before they are aware.

2. An Hypocrite is a Saint that goes by clockwork, a Machine made by the Devil's Geometry, which he winds and nicks to go as he pleases. He is the Devil's Finger-Watch, that never goes true but too fast or too slow as he sets him.

Earle, Hall, Overbury, Butler—any one of them is a mine of information and of short story suggestions to the writers of a later century.

The trick story is, in one particular, like the detective story —the more emphasis on trick, the less on characterization.

And even more than in the detective story, it is wise here for a beginner to make sure that his own mind is clear as to the difference between characterizing a figure and assigning to it certain identifying marks. Identifications have been accumulated for most of the set figures in fiction. When Frank Stockton describes the father in *The Lady or the Tiger,* ". . . a semi-barbaric king . . . a man of exuberant fancy, and, withal, of an authority so irresistible that, at his will, he turned his varied fancies into facts," he is obviously not directing his description to the purpose of making his subject come alive for the reader. He is assigning to him the customary stock-in-trade of oriental tyrants in order to make him ready for use in the plot. To bring father or princess or lover into existence would be to ruin the story; they have to remain subordinated to the trick. But when in *The Real Thing* Henry James characterizes Major and Mrs. Monarch, "It was in their faces, the blankness, the deep intellectual repose of the twenty years of country-house visiting which had given them their pleasant intonations," he is referring them to their type, but he is by no means presenting them with stock characteristics.

Rereading these two stories with attention centered on the contrasting treatments of the persons shown provides a reader with all the understanding needed concerning subordination of character in the trick story. For his own work, the writer of a trick story need only ask himself what within the story would be changed if his persons were filled out into human beings instead of being left with identifying peculiarities only. If anything would, would that change enhance the effect of the trick or detract from it?

To decide how far characterization should go in a story predominantly concerned with action is less easy. Study of two or three stories from a magazine devoted to "Westerns" in contrast with two or three from, say, some volume of Joseph Conrad's is useful here. In most of the Western stories, it will be found that the hero is limited to those stock characteristics which are all he needs for rescue of the heroine or defeat of the bandits. When his spiritual state, his fears, his self-questionings, his agony of indecision before the first shot is fired—when these become important, then the story, no matter how much action it holds, is no longer a story of action. Conrad's *Heart of Darkness* contains battle and murder and sudden death in abundance. With the narrator's interpretations taken out, there would still be left an adventure story. With the interpretations included, it is instead the story of a lost soul—no boys' book for all its high excitements and tropic splendors.

The writer who has written a story pressed full of action, and who, looking back over it, finds it wavering between two aims, has first of all to make up his mind. Does he wish chiefly to forward the action? Or does he wish to illuminate a soul? One purpose or the other must predominate. If action is to be important for itself, then the actor needs those qualities, and only those, which fit him for his performance. To give him more is to make him as ineffective as a fireman who stops to explain his attitude towards fires in front of a conflagration.

V

So far, discussion of character has proceeded as though character stood by itself. It does not in stories any more than it does in life. It never does. It stands always in relation to circumstance.

Leaving out of account the stories where character has no importance or only the slightest, we find that the relations between the person and the set of happenings in which he is enmeshed are exactly as might be foreseen; that is, they are identical with those which in life exist between the human being and his circumstances. Each given its separate paragraph, the relations are these:

The person may remain unaltered by circumstance.

The person and the circumstances surrounding him may affect each other but with the person in final control.

The person may seem to have mastered circumstance only to be outwitted by it in the end.

The person may be molded by conditions against which he struggles but which he can in no way change.

The person may be the passive recipient of happenings, battered by them but making no convincing effort against them.

The five relations have this in common—that in each the individual is the center of importance. Happenings matter or do not matter as they affect him or as they show the impossibility of his being affected. In much the greater number of stories, the persons presented fall within the second and third groups. Let us dispose first, then, of the three less usual presentations.

In the first relationship, the person is unchanged by circumstance. Circumstances, that is, loom about him, enormous, unalterable; among them walks the hero, also unalterable. Of what kind of person can this be predicated? What variety of human being walks through life, as Shadrach through the furnace, neither putting out the flames nor scorched by them?

One example is the main figure in Conrad Aiken's "Silent Snow, Secret Snow," the story of a child mind which slowly withdraws itself from the external. No alteration in the pathetic boy hero of the story is due to circumstance. Neither happenings at school nor at home, neither the presence of affection nor the pressures of family anxiety halt the march of his obsession. From beginning to end, he is altered only as alteration takes place from within—as he, or whatever secret force is at work on him, directs it. Circumstances are the frame around the picture—no more than that. When he breaks from doctor and parents to run to his own room; when, addressing his mother, the words "tore themselves from his other life suddenly, 'Mother! Mother! Go away! I hate you!'" it is from no fault of his mother's; it is in answer to no culminating outside circumstance.

A second example, though one producing a very different effect, is *Why I Live at the P.O.*, by Eudora Welty, a story which one reader may find funny to the point of laughter, another all but unbearably pathetic, but where, whatever the reader's view, he will follow an unchanging figure through the maze of family discord.

Stories of disordered minds; many stream-of-consciousness stories; some dealing with the personified trait are of this kind. Stories where an ordinary figure—not mad, not completely egoist, not shown only from beneath the shield of his own consciousness—is presented as invulnerable, are fairly sure to be based on a single extraordinary happening or on a final reversal of expectation. The effect of such a figure on the reader is not unlike the effect produced by the performance of a beach duck meeting oncoming breakers. The wave approaches; the duck neither rides it nor avoids it but, disappearing under it, reappears on the farther side, not a feather ruffled. Wave after wave roars on to its goal; the duck disappears, reappears, remains sleekly unaltered. An observer has usually two emotions, one swiftly displacing the other—first expectancy, then amused surprise. So with the reader of the story which presents normal or seemingly normal beings on whom circumstance beats unavailingly.

Two of Stacy Aumonier's stories, *Miss Bracegirdle Does Her Duty* and *The Great Unimpressionable,* are representative of the kinds of surprise provided. Led by accident to which she herself contributes no more than a momentary absence of mind, Miss Bracegirdle, impeccable spinster sister of an English curate, spends the night under the bed of a dead desperado in a strange Paris hotel. She emerges from the ordeal a little disheveled, a little discomfited, but exactly the same Miss Bracegirdle still, with no mark of experience on her. There is, in reality, no reason why a mark should be on her. She has slipped into grotesque and dangerous circumstances as she might have slipped into a puddle. She slips out from them, takes her routine morning bath, and the mud is gone. "The Great Unimpressionable" shows an English villager going through the war. The events of the war, which he can neither alter nor comprehend, leave him untouched; the death of his dog does not. He is actually, therefore, not a figure untouched by circumstance but, like all of us, one emotionally affected only by those circumstances which come within his comprehension.

Stories showing the person formed or deformed by con-

ditions against which he struggles but which he cannot overcome have been especially frequent in the twentieth century.
An example as enlightening in its presentation of minor figures as of major ones is Tess Slesinger's *Jobs in the Sky*.
Here major and minor figures alike are hypnotized by the
rush of pre-Christmas selling in a great store. Joey Andrews,
laboring joyously, half intoxicated by the mere chance to labor—"recollection of his eight months' nightmare among the
unhired was unworthy of No. 19-23, 167B of a great depart-
ment store"—is discharged at the end of the day, the Christmas rush being over. Against his will, in spite of his utmost
effort, the impersonal machinery of the store thrusts him
back to tramphood. In *70,000 Assyrians*, by William Saroyan, the paragraphs devoted to the boy Iowa show bleakly
and briefly the same struggle, the same ending to struggle.
An older example and a less desolating one is Edward Everett Hale's *The Man Without a Country*, the incidents of
which most readers can review in their own minds.

Stories in which the person is submerged by circumstance
differ from those just quoted only in that struggle, if struggle
ever existed, has ceased before the story opens. Any story of
a typical hour is necessarily the story of a person submerged
whether with his own initial consent or against it. Unless
he has been submerged, reduced to predictable action, the
hour or day chosen for presentation cannot be typical. *Not
Wanted,* by Anton Chekhov, is an example showing the difference between person struggling and person submerged.
Throughout the story, its main figure, a middle-class Rus-
sian, is continually irritated by the conditions of his life. He
complains of them, he despises them, he lifts no finger to

change them. Covering only the length of some ten hours, the story both shows those hours and compels the reader to believe that all other hours, wherever placed, will be, in effect, precisely like them. The main figure is alive, but alive only to feel, not to act.

Most Americans, however, appear to see life as a contest between man and circumstance, in which man has not yet surrendered but still feels he has a chance to control the forces pressing against him. Most writers, therefore, so depict it. Final victory may lie on one side or the other, and in the course of the contest neither man nor circumstance fails to be altered. The man is in control when he is shown as master of his essential self—not impervious to happenings but spiritually their superior. Circumstance wins when that essential self is destroyed. An example or two from life makes clear the pattern fiction follows here. History furnishes them in plenty. Sir Thomas More, jesting in his prison and on his way to death—"But say you, being higher up, am I not nearer to Heaven in this prison than in mine own house? . . . Have a care for me going up the scaffold, Master Lieutenant. I can shift for myself coming down"—is wholly master of circumstance. He dies, but he does so because of happenings his own decision has brought into being. At the other end of the scale—and still from history—Northumberland, whose attempted rebellion has ended in failure, gives happenings their start indeed, but once the start is given, he is tossed about by them, his essential self reduced to an ineffectual gelatinous quivering.

In any reader's own neighborhood, in his own family, either figure may be matched, as either is matched time and again in fiction. Hawthorne's *The Minister's Black Veil* provides an easily analyzed example of impact of happening on person, and person on happening. Here the earliest happening is the entrance of the minister, his face concealed by a black veil. He has assumed the veil in recognition of man's spiritual isolation from all his fellows—has assumed it, that is, as a result of his individual habit of thought. His wearing it puts a bar between him and his congregation, thereby enhances his isolation. This enhanced isolation brings about the next event, which event in its turn increases the isolation. So character produces happening, and produced happening reacts on character till the story comes to its foregone conclusion. As has already been pointed out, a person of any one of many temperaments and characters could substitute for the hero in *A Terribly Strange Bed* and no important alteration take place in the story. In *The Minister's Black Veil*, to exchange the minister for a being even slightly unlike in mind and spirit would be impossible. A change, even, in geography or social placing would require so many readjustments as to leave scarcely recognizable substance. This one figure, this particular figure only, is essential to there being a story at all. To this extent, *The Minister's Black Veil* resembles the stream-of-consciousness story. It differs from it in that the reader is shown landscape and minor figures—the churchyard, the congregation—directly by the author. Character and event have separate existences.

In *May Day Celebration*, by T. O. Beachcroft, the main figure, an English labor agitator, has been sharply altered by circumstance—" . . . his face, once full of fire and expression, had grown dour and set and stubborn"—but he has himself caused circumstances to be what they are. They have shaped him, but they have been given the chance to do so only at his own will. Had that will altered, circumstances must have been altered in response to the change. However malignant towards him, they are still his servants.

The wife, from whose point of observation the story is told, has also been in constant struggle, wins also a final though qualified triumph. The husband having been arrested, she remains alone in the flat.

The door closed; and she was alone.
She stood silent for a long time, thinking and seeing nothing.
Then she slowly walked to the window and pulled the curtains. How grimy they were! She sat down beside the table, which still carried the remains of tea. Many pictures of her broken and tattered life passed before her. She saw her hopes of the future torn in ragged dirty pieces, fluttering away. She knew now that she would never have a home; that from now on she need never hope for a home. The pictures of the little house she had begun to see changed to pictures of rooms in worse and worse streets; to fierce poverty, bare boards, and fireless grates, to comfortless old age.

Yet she felt calm and almost joyful. She had seen the look in Thomas's eyes. She knew he was living through the proudest and happiest moments of his whole life. She fell to thinking of the red and white cheeks, the wild black hair, he used to have. And gradually her heart grew light.*

Here again, freedom of will, freedom of choice, is left with the persons in the story. It is a limited freedom—"a drop of water in a globe of glass"—but it is freedom nonetheless.

The stories everybody has read—*William the Conqueror, The Man Who Corrupted Hadleyburg, The End of the Tether,* even a piece of folklore so intentionally fantastic as

* From *You Must Break Out Sometimes,* by T. O. Beachcroft. Published by Harper and Brothers, New York

The Devil and Daniel Webster—belong, all of them, in this category. Once the story is under way, character directs circumstance. Happenings must stop dead or change their course if character is altered.

The person who seems to have mastered circumstance but turns out at last to be its dupe, the person who fills the role of dupe but in the end is shown to be master—these are presentations found oftenest, of course, in surprise-ending stories. Kipling's *His Chance for Life,* which shows a hero inert and rabbit-like up to a given moment; John Russell's *Jetsam,* where the beachcomber hero remains spineless through twenty-seven years of his existence only to develop a spine of unusual stiffness in one day of the twenty-eighth year; Perceval Gibbon's *The Connoisseur,* the main figure of which, having tricked others, finds himself finally the most tricked of all—any reader can lengthen the list from his own reading, for the kind is a magazine favorite. Examination of any one of the stories shows, of course, that in a story of this variety there are signposts in plenty along the way if only the reader could decipher them. It shows too in almost every instance that the writer depends heavily on traditions already well established in readers' minds. In *Jetsam,* for example, the hero has Family, and English Family at that, to account for his final stiffening. In *His Chance for Life,* the appearance of the right girl accounts for abandonment of the rabbit attitude.

Wilbur Daniel Steele's *The Man Who Saw Through Heaven* is distantly related to the stories just given but escapes from trick not only through its more serious treatment of the main figure but also through use of time long enough to allow for spiritual change. The conquered becomes the conqueror not by the sudden injection of a traditional strengthener, but through prolonged travail of soul. The hero, a missionary, just married and on his way to his first foreign charge, visits an astronomer friend while waiting for the sailing of his ship, peers for the first time through the lens of a powerful telescope. The glimpse is catastrophic. It sends crashing his lifelong conception of an arranged universe, of a personal God looking from a placed Heaven straight at him. Halfway across the ocean, he goes technically "mad," escapes at a port of call and wanders desolate through Africa, seeking the God he has lost, leaving the trail of his travels by way of mud idols. When those who track him find the spot where he is buried, they find too the last idol, the re-discovered God.

The figure was crudeness itself, but . . . an attitude of interest . . . intense and static, breathless and eternal . . . penetrating to its bottom atom, to the last electron, to a hill upon it, and to a two-legged mite about to die. Marking (yes, I'll swear to the incredible) the sparrow's fall.*

Treatments of the main figure which allow him direction of circumstances throughout the story, whether resulting in his terrestrial triumph or his terrestrial destruction, call for an attitude on the part of the writer respectful of the human beings with whom he deals. Satire, mockery, the whole set of derisive attitudes, have implicit in them a belief in the power of circumstance to overcome human resistance. Which kind of story a writer produces depends less usually on his immediate will than on his inner, and often unrecognized, convictions. For in dealing with character, he can, in the main, deal with it only as he believes it to be. To read in close succession

* From *The Man Who Saw Through Heaven*. By permission of Wilbur Daniel Steele.

a dozen stories by one writer—Saroyan, Steinbeck, Kay Boyle, Eudora Welty—is to get full proof of how here even more than elsewhere in writing, a writer consistently sets down his own deep-buried convictions.

VI

To learn to put character on the page with even partial success is a task to fill most of a writer's years. It is infant-class work, however, compared with the task preceding and accompanying it—that of trying to comprehend character, to make sense out of why people act as people do act, why environment affects the one in this way, the other in that. Lack of writing skill may make a partly comprehended person stalk woodenly through the pages; lack of comprehension makes that woodenness unavoidable. How, then, is comprehension to be increased?

All the earlier part of anybody's learning is unconscious. Fra Lippo Lippi names one method traditionally effective.

> . . . when a boy starves in the streets
> Eight years together . . .
> Why, sense and soul of him alike grow sharp,
> He learns the looks of things . . .

Learning the look of things through a life lived on the edge of annihilation has undoubtedly sharpened the soul and sense of those who survived the experience—perhaps a tenth as many as have been destroyed by it—but it cannot well be a planned learning and must be an early one. Another means, also incapable of being planned and also effective, is to have grown up in a large and vocal household, where actions and motives came into lively review. Still another is to have struggled as a child through prolonged illnesses till, reading being a sole recourse, book people became real and the analyses of their actions carried over into life.

Childhood once past, however, these opportunities are past too. For an adult, there are left probably only three means capable of purposeful application.

One of these is the beating down of self-consciousness. A blanket of self-consciousness wrapped around you is as muffling as an actual blanket would be, and this whether self-consciousness take the form of shyness or of that "desire to shine" which Boswell imputes to Goldsmith. Either lessens the possibility of whole-hearted listening, whole-hearted observation. Some prolific writers, it is true, have been poor listeners, have been exhibitionists, inordinate talkers. But, in spite of exceptions, the giving of undiverted attention to the outside scene is all but a necessity to one whose preoccupation is to be with realistic fiction. Somewhere in his voluminous memoirs, H. G. Wells points out that one of his chief blessings was what he had considered a hardship at the time —his having been a young man of insignificant presence and weak, reedy voice. Nobody paid attention to him. Whether he would or would not, he was continually overlooked. Once resigned to being overlooked, he had the whole of his mind to give to others, a kind of inconspicuous recording instrument at the lower end of the dinner table.

A second means for increasing comprehension of character is consciously to encourage your own pondering on human reactions, their causes, their results.

MAN KNOCKED DOWN BY MOTOR CAR
IS KNOCKED DOWN AGAIN BY ANGRY MOTORIST.

The line is a sub-head taken from the New York *Times*. The item under the heading enlarges on it without increasing its content. The man knocked down scrambles to his feet, shouts at the advancing motorist, "It's all right! I'm not hurt." The motorist launches a blow at him—"I'll teach you to keep out of my way!"—leaps into his car and is gone.

The first response to the item is amusement, the usual first response to the incongruous, but—what made the motorist act that way? What has life done to a man, what will it do to him, whose reaction to nervous shock is fury and physical violence? Or was the fury the result of knowing himself to be in the wrong, a means of shutting off the pedestrian's justified outburst? You are still pausing over the item when an efficient reader is halfway through the paper. You are intentionally pausing, encouraging yourself to pause. To the habit of mind which lies behind all growth in understanding of character, nothing is more fatal than briskness. And the habit of not being brisk, the habit of deliberating and letting thought put down roots, is in considerable measure a cultivatable one. If you can even once shiver reponsively in answer to the shiver along that motorist's nerves as he drives veeringly towards home, swerving to miss a shadow here, swerving to miss a shadow there, justifying himself in sobbing curses, then you not only understand a little about that motorist, you are nearer to understanding a whole group of actions. You have, however, neither read your paper nor put in a restful half hour. The approaches to writing are set thick with waste.

Mr. and Mrs. John Hagen departed this week on their second honeymoon. Mr. Hagen, fifty-five, and his wife, fifty-three, were first married in 1915, were divorced in 1917, and were remarried yesterday at their son's home. Mr. Hagen is well known as the manager . . .

You stop there. You will never write a story about the Hagens. You do not want to write one. And yet—why did they do it? Why did she? What did she feel as she stood there, middle-aged, bordering on old, being united again to the man from whom she had been divorced for a generation? What had life done to her in that generation to make her willing to tolerate what once had been intolerable? Is it in the phrase "at their son's home" that the secret lies? You begin to think of her so—a woman absorbed in a small child, a woman wrapping her smothering affection around a growing boy, a woman displaced now by her son's wife. Is it her importunate need of being needed that pushes her into marriage? Whom have you known like her? What woman whose need of being needed, of preparing surprise desserts and being praised for them, of hunting out rubbers for rainy days and straw hats for sunny ones, of shaping her life around a homecoming hour, is stronger in her than any inner resource? While Mrs. Hagen is still inhabiting your mind, read Chekhov's *The Darling*. Is Mrs. Hagen that? And is Chekhov telling the truth, presenting a character; or is he pulling one thread out from the whole garment which is the person? Which do you believe? And when you have read the story for a third time, is your belief still the same?

Mrs. Hagen need not necessarily have any relation to the desolate heroine of *The Darling*. There are a dozen other things she may be, but no one of them is useful to you merely as a chance thought. It has to be a thought pursued, a thought blossoming out into mental images and stirred emotions before it becomes a help to understanding.

Next in value to the habit of deliberating over human actions, of taking time to fish for the feelings that motivated them, comes the accompanying habit of trying to turn the results of these deliberations into expressive phrases. The two processes go on together, both capable of being consciously expedited or hindered, and both preventive of that callousing of feeling, that concentration on the immediate present, so needful for the comfortable carrying on of daily life. Study of faces, with search for the words to express what the study showed; study of the relations among the members of a family; speculations on the "why" of unexpected action, with attempts to get that "why" into a sentence—these are occupations partly accidental, partly intentional, and sure to be useful to any one whose desire to write and write effectively goes deeper than a pose.

VIII

Dialogue

. . . any one of us recognizes clearly that he may know all the rules of the grammar of a foreign language, may speak the language with the correct pronunciation; but until he acquires something that is the characterizing "chant," lilt, cadence of that language, he never speaks it like a native. What distinguishes us as we come from different parts of this country is not so much the rolled *r* of the Middle Westerner or the prolonged New England *a*; it is this same rhythm and cadence of speech.

Suggested Reading

USTINOV, PETER. "A Word in the World's Ear," in *Add a Dash of Pity*. Boston: Atlantic-Little, Brown and Company.

STEINBECK, JOHN. "The Leader of the People," in *The Long Valley*. New York: The Viking Press, Compass Books.

HEMINGWAY, ERNEST. "The Killers," in *Men Without Women*. New York: Charles Scribner's Sons.

PURDY, JAMES. "Encore." *Commentary,* March 1959.

PRITCHETT, V. S. "Just a Little More," in *Stories from* The New Yorker, *1950 to 1960*. New York: Simon and Schuster.

DOYLE, SIR ARTHUR CONAN. "The Red-Headed League," in *The Adventures of Sherlock Holmes*. New York: Harper and Row.

KIPLING, RUDYARD. "William the Conqueror," in *Selected Stories from Kipling,* William Lyon Phelps, editor. New York: Doubleday and Company.

Dialogue

In the 1840's Poe wrote,

A skillful literary artist has constructed a tale. If wise, he has not fashioned his thoughts to accommodate his incidents but having conceived, with deliberate care, a certain unique or single effect to be wrought out, he then invents such incidents—he then combines such events as may best aid him in establishing this preconceived effect. If his very initial sentence tend not to the outbringing of this effect, then he has failed in his first step. In the whole composition there should be no word written of which the tendency, direct or indirect, is not to the one pre-established design.

Probably no passage in American literature has had a wider reading among would-be writers. Certainly few have received so many elucidations. And yet it is open to question whether the passage plus its elucidations has helped as many beginners at writing as it has harmed. The reason for such a question is that "single effect" has more often than not been interpreted to mean the exciting in the reader of one, and only one, emotion throughout the story. Under this interpretation, a story which is to produce horror should begin with horror, proceed to more horror, and pass from more to most. With the greater part of Poe's stories, this is exactly what they do. But a consideration of any group of memorable stories by other writers shows that the interpretation is far too limited. A story is quite as likely to produce its effect by contrast, by the juxtapositions of unlike emotions, as by emphasis upon only one. There is, however, one "single effect" which belongs to every well-conceived story. This is the effect produced upon the reader when the story is done—when he closes the book and thinks back over it. The recollection of a successful story is always predominantly colored by one emotion. The emotion may be obtained by cumulative effort, as in *The Fall of the House of Usher,* or it may come from a reinterpretation in the final paragraphs, but its presence and its kind are beyond question. Every item in a well-executed story is capable of integration when the story is recollected. And every story, whether its effect is obtained by cumulative effort or by reversal, establishes early in its course a harmony, a kind of tune, partly from its use of minor incident, partly from diction. Whatever offends against this tune is destructive to the story.

In beginners' work, the place where the tune is oftenest interrupted seems to be in dialogue. Whoever has attempted story writing—still more, whoever has read large numbers of amateur stories—knows why. To cause the figures in a story to talk is not merely to make them speak as, under the circumstances given, they probably would. It is also to make their speaking forward the action, or display the speaker's temperament or character, or elucidate the characters or temperaments or relationships of other figures in the story— or, even, to do all three. It is along with doing one or all of these that the dialogue must also carry on the tune of the story. Written sentences, therefore, can almost never be the transcript of spoken ones, in spite of the fact that a first step in learning to write dialogue is to learn to listen. After listening comes a prolonged process, usually a conscious process, of changing speech from the form in which it actually was uttered to a form which makes it appear to readers as though it had been uttered, while at the same time it performs its required work in the story.

Now and then a writer appears in whom the ability to listen is innate. Where it is not, it is fortunately one capable of cultivation. First, though, the need to cultivate it must be recognized—the exact kind of need. For listening, so far as a writer is concerned, is not a matter of getting only the sense of what is said. It is a matter of getting the swing, the pace, the individual marks of individual talk.

Except for geniuses and mimics, listeners hear usually only the substance of conversation. Even strongly marked differences between speaker and speaker are rarely heard with enough acuteness to allow for reproduction. Try writing down, without reference to books, a paragraph as spoken by some person with a foreign accent, and discover how little except the sense of the speech and perhaps an occasional striking phrase sticks in your mind. The national or racial or personal idiosyncrasies represented in your paragraph are far more likely to be idiosyncrasies learned from reading than from actual hearing. If you try to write three or four sentences as spoken by some member of your family, you will again discover that your habit in listening is to grasp the meaning of what the speaker says and to disregard in large measure his way of saying it. Probably you will never exactly copy in any story either the dialect of a given group or those lesser peculiarities which, within the group, set off one member from another. Nonetheless, listening for the tone, the tune, of talk provides the base on which written dialogue is built.

After listening, comes transcription. The Boswellian retirement to a corner to set down sentences still hot from the tongue is practicable only for a Boswell. But there are opportunities—on trains, in bus stations, in the family living-room—first for listening, then for the immediate exact recording of successive sentences informally spoken. These are opportunities to be used not once but again and again. Transcription and more transcription and still more, even of the veriest scraps of talk, is valuable as a preliminary to writing. The sentences transcribed will not, perhaps, be used in any story on which the writer is immediately at work, quite possibly not in any later story; but the value of the setting down does not lie in its producing immediate story material. It lies in teaching the transcriber how sentences actually are spoken, what must happen to them when they are transferred to the page. The woman who summarized her writing difficulties, "The trouble with my stories is that I can't seem to think up anything to write about and I can't make my people talk," was perhaps a woman meant for some profession other than writing, but in her second admission she was naming a difficulty by no means only hers. Successfully changing spoken dialogue into written is usually one of the latest of a beginner's conquests.

Of the changes to be made, the first, of course, is compression. Talk exactly recorded is talk redundant to the point of absurdity. It blocks the story, leaves no room for anything but talk. Sinclair Lewis has an especial talent for writing dialogue which gives the impression of falling from the speaker's lips loose and full and exactly as spoken. Yet comparison of any passage he has written with the actual conversation of persons such as those displayed shows how cunningly he makes one word do the work of three, one sentence the work of a dozen.

"Just been making a trip through the South. Business conditions not very good down there," said one of the council.

"Is that a fact? Not very good, eh?"

"No, didn't strike me they were up to normal."

"Not up to normal, eh?"

"No, I wouldn't hardly say they were."

The whole council nodded sagely and decided, "Yump, not hardly up to snuff."

"Well, business conditions ain't what they ought to be out West neither, not by a long shot."

"That's a fact. And I guess the hotel business feels it. That's one good thing, though; these hotels that've been charging five bucks a day—yes, and maybe six-seven—for a rotten room are going to be darn glad to get four, and maybe give you a little service."

"That's a fact. Say, uh, speaking about hotels, I hit the St. Francis at San Francisco for the first time the other day, and, say, it certainly is a first-class place."

"You're right, brother! The St. Francis is a swell place—absolutely A-1."

"That's a fact. I'm right with you. It's a first-class place." *

The loquacity of the group, the repetitiousness, the tiresomeness are achingly evident. The sense of the talk's going on interminably, folding and refolding itself about the same topics, is fully conveyed. And yet the reading time is of the briefest. How the effect is created, how much of it comes from subject matter and how much from wording, is worth any beginner's study. It is worth it not only in the passage

* From *Babbitt*, by Sinclair Lewis. Copyright, 1922, by Harcourt, Brace and Company, Inc.

given but still more in those conversations he seeks out and sets down for himself and later tries to reduce, without loss of effect, from three pages to one.

Compression, however, is only the first of the needed changes. Observe the following question and answer, taken down exactly from the lips of two speakers unconscious of audience.

"Who's t' go? Got 'ny idea?"
"I do' know. No' un fr' here s' far as I've heard. O'course, meeting in Bahs'n . . ."

Illiterates? No, philologists discussing a prospective meeting of the Modern Language Association. In casual conversation, all speakers slur vowels, drop final consonants, take short cuts through syntax. The result is that, so far as the reader is concerned, speech put on the page as it falls from the lips of the speaker sends that speaker sliding precipitously down the social scale. Not only does what he says require trimming to fit the space allotted to it, it has also to be dressed out with those final "g's" and central "t's" which every tongue neglects. If exact transcription had no other value, it would still be worth while for pointing out the effect of unaltered reproduction on an imaginary person's social standing.

Even the writing of dialect is never actually a reproduction. It is moderated in behalf of the reader, who is willing to pay just so much toll and no more for the privilege of being introduced to strange scenes and persons. In *Child of God*, by Roark Bradford, Willie, the childlike colored hero, comments,

"Cap'm Archie say he gonter bring me a ten-cent cigar to go walkin' up de gallows wid in my mouf'. . . . An' I makes me a speech up yonder—"

The marks of a negro speaker are on the sentences, but no word is even momentarily unintelligible. James Still, in his presentations of Southern hill people, is as economical. Mother had said,

"A house proper to raise chaps in, a cellar for laying by food, and lasty neighbors. Now, that aint asking for the moon ball."

Elsie Singmaster, with her Pennsylvania Dutch, is still more sparing, using inversions and an occasional oddity of phrase, but keeping well within the limits of easy comprehension. Dialect on the page, as contrasted with dialect on the tongue, accomplishes its end by suggestion of difference rather than by presentation of it.

By strict interpretation, every human who speaks, speaks dialect. No one is free from racial and local speech marks, whether the "different to" of the Englishman as against the "different from" of the American, or the forthright r's of the Rockies in contrast with the absentee r's of Virginia. For a writer, however, the problem is only what special marks and how many or few of them must be put on paper for the sake of characterization, or for differentiating one person or group from the rest. Every mark is paid for by a fragment of extra effort on the reader's part. Unless it accomplishes a purpose, it is not worth paying for. And with dialect as with the speech which falls short of dialect, what the individual would actually have said has to be lightened, corrected, rearranged to bring it from mouth to page without exaggeration of its special quality.

But after the manner of an imaginary person's speech has shown his race or his nationality, his social position, his character, it has still its other task to do; in one fashion or another it must advance the story. Observe the uses of the four conversations that follow.

1. "Mr. Claridge," Hewitt proceeded slowly, "when did you first find that Lord Stanway's cameo was a forgery?"

Claridge literally bounced in his chair. His face paled but he managed to stammer sharply, "What—what—what d'you mean? Forgery? Do you mean to say I sell forgeries? Forgery? It wasn't a forgery!"

"Then," continued Hewitt, "if it wasn't a forgery, why did you destroy it and burst your trap door and desk to imitate a burglary?" . . .

"Destroy it? What—what—I didn't—didn't destroy it!"

"Threw it in the river, then—don't prevaricate about details."
                    —Arthur Morrison, *The Stanway Cameo Mystery**

2. Last time he had come to see her, Basil had worn a rose in his buttonhole. How handsome he had looked in that bright blue suit, with that dark red rose! . . .

"The headmaster's wife keeps asking me to dinner. It's a perfect nuisance. I never get an evening to myself in that place."

"But can't you refuse?"

"Oh, well, it doesn't do for a man in my position to be unpopular."

                    —Katherine Mansfield, *The Singing Lesson***

3. . . . one evening there was a little scene. Laura suddenly snapped out:

* From *Martin Hewitt Investigates*, by Arthur Morrison
** From *The Garden Party*, by Katherine Mansfield. By permission of Alfred A. Knopf, publisher

"Please don't keep looking at me, Mother." And Mrs. Kinghorn, with a frightened, startled expression, said:

"I'm not looking at you, darling, I'm reading my book."

"Oh, no, you're not. You are watching me all the time."

"Watching you, dearie? What should I be watching you for? I'll go upstairs if you'd rather."

"Oh, no, of course not. I'm going out soon."

Then Mrs. Kinghorn said quietly, "It's quite natural."

"What is?" asked Laura.

"That I should irritate you both. Don't think I don't understand."

"There's nothing to understand," Laura cried, exasperated to madness, jumping to her feet. "Only we can't escape you, John and I. It's a dreadful feeling that somebody is watching you every minute of the day and night."

"Don't I know it?" said Mrs. Kinghorn cheerfully. "It was just the same with me when I was engaged to Richard. Richard's mother meant well, and I mean well, but until you're married, you'll find me tiresome. The sooner you're married, the better."

"What are you going to do then?" asked Laura.

"Oh, I'll be all right. Don't worry about me." She pushed her skinny hand through her short sunset hair. "Don't worry about me, darling. I'll be quite all right in some little place by myself."

Laura, in a perfect passion, answered, "Oh, why will you be so good and so self-sacrificing? Why don't you say something mean or spiteful?"

Mrs. Kinghorn answered placidly, "I dare say I could be mean and spiteful if I tried. Most women can," and went on with her book.

— Hugh Walpole, *Mother's a Pity**

4. "We should begin," said my father, turning himself half round in bed, and shifting his pillow a little towards my mother's, as he opened the debate,—"We should begin to think, Mrs. Shandy, of putting this boy into breeches."

* In *Collier's Magazine*, January 8, 1938. Used by permission of Eric S. Pinker and Adrienne Morrison, Inc., author's agents

"We should so," said my mother.

"We defer it, my dear," quoth my father, "shamefully."

"I think we do, Mr. Shandy," said my mother.

"Not but the child looks extremely well," said my father, "in his vest and tunic."

"He looks very well in them," replied my mother.

"And for that reason it would be almost a sin," added my father, "to take him out of 'em."

"It would so," said my mother. . . .

"When he gets these breeches made," cried my father in a higher tone, "he'll look like a beast in 'em."

"He will be very awkward in them at first," replied my mother.

"They should be of leather," said my father. . . .

"They will last him," said my mother, "the longer.". . .

"I am resolved, however," said my father—"he shall have no pockets in them."

"There is no occasion for any," said my mother.

"I mean in his coat and waistcoat," cried my father.

"I mean so too," replied my mother.

"Though if he gets a gig or top—Poor souls! It is a crown and sceptre to them—they should have where to secure it."

"Order it as you please, Mr. Shandy," replied my mother.

"But don't you think it right?" added my father, pressing the point home to her.

"Perfectly," said my mother, "if it pleases you, Mr. Shandy."

"There's for you!" cried my father, losing temper. "Pleases me!"

> —Laurence Sterne, *The Life and Opinions of Tristram Shandy, Gentleman.*

In the first excerpt, what we get from the dialogue is fact, evidence accumulated by one person and offered to the reader through the medium of another.

In the second, Basil's speech is the writer's device for injuring him in the reader's opinion.

In *Mother's a Pity,* the relation between mother and daughter, the cause of that relation, and its temporary nature are implicit in a dialogue which, so far as concerns the words actually set down, reveals only a thwarted attempt at a quarrel.

The excerpt from *Tristram Shandy,* which outwardly is a discussion of putting a child into breeches, is for the reader a character analysis of two persons and a portrayal of the relation of one to the other.

The dialogues given thus far have been, in the main realistic, the writers forming the speeches of their persons to sound in the readers' ears like actual speech. Things said and way of saying have been directed towards producing an illusion of reality. Few readers need to be reminded that the illusion of reality is not always the illusion sought. Dunsany, Wodehouse, Cabell and a host of others emphasize the point. "People don't talk that way," is an accusation which has standing against the realistic story only and only a limited standing then. Beyond being intelligible, dialogue need have nothing to do with actuality. What it does have to do with —to state the point yet again—is the tune of the story, the special harmony the author has set himself to maintain. In *Jeeves and the Unbidden Guest,* Bertie Wooster, in his capacity of reluctant host, goes with Jeeves to the front door, there to find the visitor lying on the mat.

"He's had some sort of dashed fit," I said. I took another look. "Jeeves! Someone's been feeding him meat!"

"Sir?"

"He's a vegetarian, you know. He must have been digging into a planked steak or something. Call up a doctor!"

"I hardly think it will be necessary, sir. If you would take his lordship's legs, while I—"

"Great Scott, Jeeves! You don't think—he can't be—"

"I'm inclined to think so, sir."

And by Jove, he was right. Once on the right track, you couldn't mistake it. Motty was under the surface.

It was the deuce of a shock.

"You never can tell, Jeeves!"

"Very seldom, sir."

"Remove the eye of authority and where are you?"

"Precisely, sir."

"Where is my wandering boy tonight and all that sort of thing, what!"

"It would seem so, sir."

"Well, we had better bring him in, eh?"

"Yes, sir."

.   .   .   .

Next morning . . . I went to Motty's room to investigate . . .

"What ho!" I said.

"What ho!" said Motty.

"What ho! What ho!"

"What ho! What ho! What ho!" *

Nobody believes or is expected to believe that Bertie or Jeeves or Motty or any other human beings would actually talk in the fashion given. But the glittering absurdity, the breathless circus-ring mirthfulness of the story, is strengthened by it. So with many of the exchanges of speech in Mark Twain's *The Man Who Corrupted Hadleyburg*. So, to an end quite different, the rolling periods in Cabell's early stories.

Then these three princes rose and knelt before the priest; they were clad in long bright garments, and they glittered with gold

* From *Carry On, Jeeves,* by P. G. Wodehouse, copyright, 1916, reprinted by permission from Doubleday, Doran and Company, Inc.

and many jewels. He standing among them shuddered in his sombre robe. "Hail, King of England!" cried these three.

"Hail, ye that are my kinsmen!" he answered: "hail, ye that spring of an accursed race, as I! And woe to England for that hour wherein Manuel of Poictesme held traffic with the Sorceress of Provence, and the devil's son begot an heir for England! Of ice and of lust and of hell-fire are all we sprung; and old records attest it; and fickle and cold and ravenous and without shame are all our race until the end. Of our brother's dishonor ye make merchandise today, and today fratricide whispers me, and leers, and Heaven help me! I attend."

—James Branch Cabell, *The Satraps**

The belief that dialogue is conversation transferred to paper, is one to get rid of early. "That is the way they did talk" is no more an excuse for pointless printed speech than "That is what did happen" is an excuse for implausible action.

But the fact that written dialogue is more than transcribed talk having been first grasped and later enforced by reading and listening, what are you, a beginner at writing, to do to improve the dialogue in your own stories? Means of general improvement have already been named. You are to listen and to continue to listen. You are to write down conversation exactly and then to re-work what you have written until, having ceased to be the thing you heard, it has come instead to appear upon the page as though it were that thing. These two processes are for the good of your future writing. For the story you have in hand, all you can do is to isolate and interrogate the dialogue passages. What do you want a particular piece of dialogue to do? Is it to carry information, elucidate character, enhance the story's mood? Does it have

* By permission of Robert M. McBride and Company, publishers

the right sound when read aloud? Are its tone and diction similar to those of other passages by the same speaker? Finally, is it worth the space it takes?

"I ain't going," said Julia. "Well, that's enough for you, ain't it? I tell yuh I don't want to go.". . .

.   .   .   .

"Why should I?" Julia asked, looking away from him. "You didn't want me. You wanted her. You asked me only because you thought you had to."

In the story from which the two passages just quoted are taken, three pages separate them, but three pages are not enough, all the pages in the story are not enough, to allow for Julia's transformation. That transformation is not the result of her saying "ain't" on one page and avoiding it on another nor yet of the "yuh" which makes its appearance in the third sentence. The essential difference is in the ring of the sentences. Consistency can come only from the writer's sufficiently realizing the presented person so that he is conscious of shock when the speaker steps out of one character into another.

As in many other places, acting out a scene will sometimes help. When you speak his words aloud, does the person on page one sound on page five like the same person? Do his sentences, as you pronounce them, have likenesses which mark them as his? Placed in the situation and addressing the listener that has been provided for him, would the speaker speak as he does? In the same rounded sentences, in the same full paragraphs? Or does his maker know, as soon as he reads the paragraphs aloud, that no listener would passively receive those solid ammunition rounds of information or opinion?

Another point to be kept clearly in mind is that no dialogue, spoken or written, is ever made up exclusively of words. Watch the unspoken interruptions which break in on even the most solid blocks of talk. One speaker may speak steadily for minutes. Nonetheless, his speech is continually interrupted. He turns, gesticulates, hesitates. His listener, saying nothing, evinces agreement, boredom, anger. In actual person-to-person talk almost never is the listener a recipient only. Almost never does the speaker say all he has to say in words. When your sister said of a newcomer, "Yes, he's certainly good-looking, and he always has plenty to say for himself," how did you know, as surely as if she had proclaimed it, that she disliked the man? In this particular story on which you are working, how can you put on paper, either in the sentences themselves or in their accompanying tags, what will make a reader know that "he's good-looking" means "I detest him"?

IX

Verbal Revision

"Miser of sound and syllable, no less than Midas of his coinage."

The word, the pigment of the poet's art,
The word, that speaks the fulness of the heart,
The wingéd word, like arrow to the goal,
Stinging to action the lethargic soul,
The current word, the idiom of the street,
The coin of quick exchange with all we meet;
The fitting word, high culture's final test;
The pungent word of graphic tale and jest,
The flavoring lemon in the punch of wit,
So apt—and yet so easy *not* to hit . . .

I sing the word beginning once with God,
Milestone of backward road from man to clod.

Melville   Best   Anderson
in *The Happy Teacher.*

Verbal Revision

I

"SCULPTURE is easy. All you do is take a piece of marble and knock off what you don't want."

The ways of statue making have altered since that misleading sentence was written, but the application of the sentence to writing has not. For in the same fashion, writing is easy. You dip your hand into the reservoir of words, bring up the ones you want and shake the unwanted ones off your fingers. In each instance, though, the difficulty is the same. What you do want is not to be determined until the knocking off and shaking off are all but completed. Nearly every story in its early drafts distorts itself by unnecessary words —this quite apart from unnecessary detail or contradictory action. If five words in a sentence can be made to do the work of ten, then time and again—though by no means always—ten can do twice what they at first were doing. And one of the unchangeable facts a writer always faces is that he can have only so many words in any story.

How many "so many" may be differs from story to story, but one condition remains true in all but the rarest instances. The "so many" is never so many as the writer uses in the beginning, never so many as in the beginning he feels he must use. Cutting merely for reduction of bulk is a form of revision rarely to be avoided. And this reduction is made not only, or even chiefly, with an eye on editorial limitations. It is made in order that the story may be intelligible enough, concise enough, to allow readers to follow it to its conclusion.

Cutting to reduce bulk is, of course, only one of the several kinds of verbal revision. There is revision to improve sound, there is revision to clear up meaning and enforce sense. The various kinds are carried on consciously or unconsciously, at every stage of writing except the earliest. Any experienced writer recalls hovering over his pages with "a necessary fact in hand and nowhere to put it down." Every writer recalls too instances of balancing between two expressions, putting in one, taking it out, putting in the other, returning to the first. To a considerable extent, it is this balancing, this persistent weighing and re-weighing of tiny blocks, that constitutes the final difference between the story almost anybody might have put together and the story that one hand only could have shaped.

For the unaccustomed writer, however, even though some revision does go on at nearly all stages, it is usually wise to leave intensive polishing till the story is entirely on paper. In the course of writing, that much praised "infinite capacity for taking pains" degenerates readily into mere piddling, till what the writer believes to be a struggle towards perfection becomes no more than a delaying action against the effort of further invention. Once the story is all on paper, its more obvious excrescences cut away, there comes then the period for close study, phrase-by-phrase study, of wording.

The earliest verbal revision is usually that concerned with the elimination of individual words. Most of such elimination, it is true, has to be done by feel, not by rule; but there exist words and phrases which, even when the writer himself finds no fault with them, yet are suspect by reason of their confirmed habit of being superfluous.

Before he begins writing, a writer has ordinarily some intuition about how long his whole story should be. His idea, he expects, should carry thus many or thus many words for its expression, will run thin, will shape up lumpily, if that number be much exceeded. In the early drafts, that number is exceeded, with the result that the story does exactly what was expected of it. By this time, however, its maker is enamoured of his phrases, no one of them seeming to him unnecessary, none clumsy, none misplaced.

A first help in finding which actually are wrongly placed is time. A story as far finished as its writer can finish it and then cooled by a week's or a month's neglect shows sometimes, when it is brought to light, whole paragraphs removable. A second help is exploration, a few pages at a time, with attention fixed at each reading upon one of the special weaknesses to which beginners are liable. One of these weaknesses is the use of adjectives, and especially the use of them in descriptive passages.

As the full circle of the moon passed behind its mourning veil of clouds, the garden was shrouded in shaggy palms clustered in motionless groups, standing guard in the pathless wilderness that pressed close around the hacienda. Shiny-leaved banana trees no longer shimmered in the intermittent moonlight. The incessant croaking of tree frogs ceased abruptly. Birds waited softly in their nests. The garden was uneasily silent, as if all nature were holding its breath. Beneath the oppressive stillness, the pounding of rebellious tides from the coast vibrated in slow ominous undertones, a muffled throbbing beneath the languorous mobility of the tropics.

The morning sunshine broke gaily over the low mists and showed the rocky cliffs emerging out of the white foggy depths like grim Titans. Hardly distinguishable from the natural eminences, the grey towers of a castle loomed.

No one reading this book is likely to have been guilty of a passage so bad as either of the ones above. Lesser sins of the same nature, however, are all but invariable in unrevised manuscripts. A few of the more usual ones appear in the sentences below.

A white swan floated on the still water.
In answer, a tall six-foot man got up from his chair.
Green trees crowded close on the blue water.
Around him, tall trees seemed to brush the sky.
The light revealed wet, mossy walls, with water trickling from top to bottom of them.

What the writer of each of these sentences is doing is, of course, translating a visual image into words. What he fails to realize is that one of the words he uses is implicit in the other. "A white swan"—swans are white; when you think of a swan, whiteness is part of your thought. A black swan is worth the adjective. So is a red-wing blackbird. So is a white crow. So are brown trees or grey water. But when color, form, size, quality are the accustomed ones, they require no special mention. The awkward hippopotamus, the lumbering bear, the white lily—it is not because the adjectives are trite that they are ridiculous; they are ridiculous because they are already tacitly expressed in the noun they accompany. And when an accompanying adjective says of the noun only what that noun can say unaided, a place has been discovered for word economy. Ordinarily, too, the economy brings about improvement other than that of saving space. "A swan floated on the still water." "Around him, trees seemed to brush the sky"—either is more effective without its modifier.

"Wet, mossy walls, with water trickling from top to bottom of them"—try in your imagination to send water trickling from bottom to top. It is a feat not lightly accomplished. An early step in the verbal revision of any first draft is to go through the draft, page by page, and not too many pages at a sitting, looking for doubled statements, for statements false or obvious.

But that the meaning of one word is implicit in another does not always mean that either should go. A phrase is not necessarily useless merely because it can be removed without impairment of sense. Its usefulness may be for something quite other than sense—for sound, for emphasis, for delay. Pater's dictum, "All art doth but consist in the removal of surplusage," is as safe a guide as on the day he wrote it, but the question of what is surplusage is no more answered now than it was then. Consider the two sentences below.

 . . . a tall, six-foot man got up from his chair.
I pushed the button on my flash; a yellow, Chinese face was within a foot of my own.

Is "tall" in the first sentence superfluous? Almost certainly, yes. Is "yellow" in the second? Almost certainly, no. Chinese faces are yellow as regularly as swans are white, but the two words "yellow," "Chinese," give to the reader the two quick yet distinct shocks of recognition felt by the teller. Much more than meaning must be considered in any revision. If Pater's sentence had read "Art consists in removing surplusage," it would have crowded its full sense into half the words, but it would also have slain its chances of survival.

Along with descriptive modifiers, attention should go also to those qualifying modifiers from which over-use has squeezed much of the virtue—*very*, for example, and *quite* and *rather*.

"Remarkable!" Aubrey muttered, staring at the painting.
"Very remarkable!" Aubrey muttered, staring at the painting.
"Quite remarkable!" Aubrey muttered, staring at the painting.

If the writer's purpose is to show Aubrey really impressed by that painting, then the solitary word best serves his purpose. And it is worth any writer's while—*quite* worth his while, *very* worth his while—to observe the shade of meaning added in either case by the additional word.

But even when modifiers actually modify, readers tire of the continuous tagging of noun and verb.

The little stream wound sparklingly down through the tiny valley towards the shaded pool in which its murmuring course was finally lost.

Here, no matter how appropriate the individual modifiers, one and only one joined to each noun and verb cannot fail to make the sentence disagreeable. Repeated alterations of the beat of sentences is always necessary.

After modifiers, connectives are the single words most in need of watching. *And* and *so* are the chief offenders. *And* is necessarily one of the most frequently used words in the language. Its obtrusive repetition is usually no more than a sign of mental laziness on the part of the writer.

The night air was cool and fresh, *and* Marian took a deep breath. She was glad she had arranged to have a taxi waiting for her at the foot of the driveway *and* hoped it would be there on time. She wrapped her cape around her *and* walked stealthily down the road. The taxi was waiting near the hedge, *and* Marian stepped into it with the air of a conqueror.

The repetition is as monotonous as the droning of a fly; presently it is as irritating. Removal of half the *and's,* even with no other change, would work improvement.

Repeated *and's,* however, may be used in fashions by no means monotonous.

. . . and ran into the room and fell upon my knees before her and kissed her hands and dress and shoes and sobbed out my relief and pain and futile longing . . .

Every reader can recall other passages like this one where *and,* used and re-used, sends the sentence hurrying along the page. These are uses quite different, though, from the tying together of one clause and then one more clause.

An overused *so,* that first recourse of feeble minds, has nothing to recommend it unless it is used as a means of characterization in dialogue or first-person telling.

She was afraid he would come and talk to her, so she went into the house.
They pulled the rope tight so it would not slip.
Burt knew the road, so they got safely to the first stopping place.

Minor reasons could be adduced against the use of *so* in any of the three sentences given, but the major reasons lie in the failure of the sentences to assert importances over unimportances and in the awkwardness of their sound.

Modifiers and connectives having been looked to, subordinate clauses come next under scrutiny, especially those beginning with *which*.

The color of the house was a dull grey, which gave it a sullen, dark appearance which was distasteful to her.

The signpost which he had seen first had pointed in a different direction from the second one, which confused him a good deal.

A sound which was scarcely distinct enough to be heard roused him from the reverie which had been absorbing him.

Stumbling up the stairs to his room, which was on the second floor, he realized . . .

The first, second, and third of the sentences given above each contain two *which's;* each *which* in each sentence possesses a separate antecedent. If such an arrangement makes for effectiveness, there is, of course, no reason why it should not be used, but a sentence so provided has ordinarily a pair of drawbacks. It sets a *which* and a *which* (as ugly a word as language holds) neighboring on each other; and it raises to the importance of a clause what a modifier or a phrase could express even better.

The color of the house, a dull grey, gave it a sullen, dark appearance distasteful to her.

There are other forms for the statement, according to whether the writer's purpose is to emphasize the dreary look or the effect of that look upon the person. No one of the forms, though, demands a duplication of *which's.*

—which confused him a good deal.

Here the *which* has its antecedent only in the general idea of
the clause preceding, not in a particular word. Again, the
pronouncement against such a usage is a pronouncement
only, not a ukase. There exist sentences demanding a loose
which and profiting by it. But in his own work a writer is
called on to look twice at *which's* thus dangling. Now and
then his sentence demands it; oftener what demands it is his
own unwillingness to labor on the reshaping of the sentence.

A sound which was scarcely distinct enough to be heard roused
him from the reverie which had been absorbing him.

Should both the *which's* be removed? Or is one needed for
placing of emphasis? What arrangement of words will put a
chief importance on "sound"? What will give "reverie" importance?

With the fourth example, we take it for granted that
"second-floor" has something to do with the situation and
therefore must be retained. Observe the sentence, then, in
five forms.

Stumbling up the stairs to his room, which was on the second
floor, he realized . . .
Stumbling up the stairs to his room—which was on the second
floor—he realized . . .
Stumbling up the stairs to his room on the second floor . . .
Stumbling up the stairs to his second-floor room . . .
Stumbling up to his second-floor room . . .

More often than not, sentences made by an inexpert hand
are overloaded with clauses as well as with modifiers. To reduce clause to phrase, phrase to single word, saves space and
concentrates meaning. There are sentences where, for the

sake of sound or emphasis, the clause, though readily reducible, should still remain a clause, but no inexperienced writer can afford to take it for granted that his own rotund sentences are among them.

Three-fourths of verbal revision is elimination. The other fourth goes to strengthening of the words that remain. With modifiers reduced in number, nouns and verbs carry a greater weight, and therefore require a more careful selection. The colorless verb especially needs to be looked to in nearly all amateur writing. It can, of course, be over-colored. J. J. Montague's burlesque of contemporary stylistic prose —" 'Don't kiss me,' she insincered. 'Why not?' he curioused. 'Because—' she uneasied."—is both a warning and a guide. The conspicuous use of verbs in which adverbs are implicit is unfortunate, as is any conspicuous struggle for effect, but "she said insincerely," "he asked curiously," "she answered uneasily" makes quite as hard reading.

How much of the work of the sentence, then, may the verb do? How much does it do with the notable short story writers? Note the effects obtained in the sentences following —not, it may be pointed out, sentences by beginners.

Freen fidgeted around the room. He pawed over the books on the table, the sheet music on the piano. Finally his anxiety blustered out into words.

"And then that boy, that young ——" The sudden drop of his voice elided the epithet. "That boy" was prancing down the veranda towards them.

From a book on etiquette he exhumed a miscellany of useful and peculiar wisdom.

A sound squeezed itself through the silence.

—— rushed us aft together, gripped as we were, screaming "Murder!" like a lot of lunatics . . . And the ship running for her life, touch and go all the time.

These are sentences containing no extraordinary or fanciful uses of words. Any reader can select similar sentences. Considering the examples—the ones here given or his own— he must recognize the compactness, the sense of movement, given to a sentence by a verb which suggests at once the action and its quality or cause. Not many writers are better at this suggestiveness than Henry James. Observe the verbs and their modifiers in the passage following.

"I've come from Mr. Rivet," the lady said at last . . .

"Ah, Claude Rivet recommended me?" I inquired; and I added that it was very kind of him, though I could reflect that, as he only painted landscape, this was not a sacrifice.

The lady looked very hard at the gentleman, and the gentleman looked around the room. Then, staring at the floor a moment and stroking his mustache, he rested his pleasant eyes on me with the remark: "He said you were the right one."

"I try to be, when people want to sit."

"Yes, we should like to," said the lady anxiously.

"Do you mean together?"

My visitors exchanged a glance. "If you could do anything with *me*, I suppose it would be double," the gentleman stammered.

"Oh, yes, there's naturally a higher charge for two figures than for one."

"We should like to make it pay," the husband confessed.

"That's very good of you," I returned, appreciating so unwonted a sympathy—for I supposed he meant pay the artist.

A sense of strangeness seemed to dawn on the lady. "We mean for the illustrations—Mr. Rivet said you might put one in."

"Put one in—an illustration?" I was equally confused.

"Sketch her off, you know," said the gentleman, coloring . . .

"Ah, you're—you're—a—?" I began, as soon as I had mastered my surprise. I couldn't bring out the dingy word "models"; it seemed to fit the case so little.

"We haven't had much practice," said the lady.

"We've got to *do* something, and we've thought that an artist in your line might perhaps make something of us," her husband threw off. He further mentioned that they didn't know many artists and that they had gone first, on the off-chance (he painted views, of course, but sometimes put in figures—perhaps I remembered) to Mr. Rivet, whom they had met a few years before at a place in Norfolk where he was sketching.

"We used to sketch a little ourselves," the lady hinted.

"It's very awkward, but we absolutely *must* do something," her husband went on.

"Of course, we're not so *very* young," she admitted, with a wan smile.*

At the other end of the scale from Henry James is Hemingway. Practicing an economy as complete though entirely different in kind, he sends his repeated *said's* shooting like bullets across the page. In *The Killers,* two gangsters have taken possession of a lunchroom, waiting for their prospective victim to enter and talking meanwhile with the counter boy.

"All right," George said. "What are you going to do with us afterward?"

"That'll depend," Max said. "That's one of those things you never know at the time."

George looked up at the clock. It was a quarter past six. The door from the street opened. A streetcar motorman came in.

"Hello, George," he said. "Can I get supper?"

* From *The Real Thing and other Stories,* by Henry James. By permission of The Macmillan Company, publishers

"Sam's gone out," George said. "He'll be back in about half an hour."

"I'd better go up the street," the motorman said. George looked at the clock. It was twenty minutes past six.

"That was nice, bright boy," Max said. "You're a regular little gentleman."

"He knew I'd blow his head off," Al said from the kitchen.

"No," said Max. "It ain't that. Bright boy is nice. He's a nice boy. I like him."

At six-fifty-five George said: "He's not coming." *

The suave irony of the first passage, the bantering and callous ferocity of the second—neither, naturally, lies entirely in the verbs. The arrangement of the words, the adjectives or the conspicuous lack of adjectives—these and other sentence elements must also be taken into consideration. But to a considerable degree, the verbs themselves are responsible for the tone achieved. A non-writer's favorite reply here is, "But you cannot contrast the two pieces of writing. The writers were trying to do different things." They were; but, whatever they were trying to do, words were their medium. Anyone familiar with stories badly written will recall scenes of desperate action, scenes of supposed suavity, which, alike, lie flat on the page, lines of written syllables and no more. Along with emotional and intellectual responses to story material must go always the placing and replacing of words to make them express those responses.

But though the weaknesses of certain word uses are evident enough when they are pointed out in a given sentence, how are you to be sure of them when they are not pointed

* From *Men Without Women,* by Ernest Hemingway. By permission of Charles Scribner's Sons, publishers.

out? How are you to find them in your own work? If you are a newcomer to writing, probably it is best to put your earliest efforts on other people's sentences. What of the *and's* and *so's,* the *which's* and *very's* and the descriptive adverbs and adjectives in the sentences below—sentences, all of them, clipped from the stories of amateurs? How far, merely by removing some of the words from a sentence, can you improve it? How far can you improve it by altering the order of the remaining words?

1. It was late one August night when she knocked at our door.

2. A deep breath now and then and the occasional shifting of some weary body on the hard rough flooring was all that disturbed the uncommunicative mood that seemed to have fallen on the few derelict humans seeking shelter there.

3. Sprawling roots curled around his feet like coiled creatures as he stumbled through the rough-barked trees, interlaced with unresisting vines.

4. We had spent seven consecutive summers at Laguna, which made it hard now for us to give up going again.
Mother had just about given up the whole idea of finding a house, and was beginning to think of ways in which she could reconcile us to staying in town for the next three months, when Joan and I decided to do some very vigorous house-hunting on our own, for we were quite determined to find a place.

5. The river rolled very smoothly onward and swirled in innumerable patterns around twigs and rocks which it carried along in its easy, effortless current toward the security of the open sea.

6. Several minutes passed, while various members of her party tried to persuade her, and finally she allowed herself to be led off through the doorway leading into the lobby. The curtain dropped

to show a passage of fifteen minutes, and, as it rose again, the scene was the same as before.

Remember, as you read these examples, that there is no such thing as one inevitably right form for any sentence. There are only forms more or less clear, more or less forceful, more or less pleasant to eye and ear. Remember too that when a particular word in a sentence is wrong, it is not because of grammarians' pronouncements against it but because it confuses sense or wastes space or produces unpleasantness in sound. If it does not do these things, it ceases to be wrong, for grammar and syntax are not dictators over language but only recorders of its reputable uses. Each, however, is a recorder worth attention. "Mere grammar is twisted into the nature of the language about as mere gravitation is twisted into that of the physical universe," and an eye on mere grammar will prevent both some unconscious awkwardnesses and some of those which the perpetrator has fondly thought of as "style." Not many people need consciously concern themselves with style at any time. None need do so till after a decent mastery is attained over the tools of the writing trade. Clarity, compactness, exactitude—these being attained, what lies beyond them is so wholly an expression of the individual writer's taste and attitude that general counsel is useless.

Verbal revision, however, is one of the processes in writing —one of the few—wherein amateurs can sometimes help one another. Amateur help is frequently over-positive, frequently erratic, but in the pursuit of superfluous modifiers, clauses wrongly subordinated, tiresome repetitions, almost any reader with a sound grammar-school training, with enough feeling for the language to want to write, and enough honesty to say what he thinks, can be of use to a beginner.

II

"In an inexplicable suicide, for which there is no known motive . . ."

San Francisco Chronicle

Taking out the unnecessary parts from a set of sentences is sometimes all that is needed for turning bad writing into good. This disburdening, however, is not necessarily limited to the removal of words, discussed in the preceding section, or to the cutting off of clauses repetitious to absurdity, as in the sentence given above. Quite as often, it can be accomplished only by a clarification of the writer's thought in regard either to the material of his story or to his reader's approach to the story.

1. Several times that night Johnson expected the old man to die, but he clung doggedly to life with a strange persistence.

2. She suffered intensely in her child's suffering, because she loved him with the devotion which mothers give to their children.

3. Sitting out dances made her unhappy, for she did not like to be neglected.

Any one of the three statements is an assault on the reader's intelligence, for in each the maker of the sentence has turned the general into the particular, presenting a universal condition as though it were a special case.

An assault on the reader's intelligence too is the overloading not only of a sentence with words but of a passage with details.

1. The rancid odor of grease nauseated him as he opened the heavy door; he heard the familiar whining cry of a hungry child. With a feeble gesture of disgust . . .

2. He recognized the old rowboat floundering, waterlogged, on a greyish patch of filthy sand, the small dirty wharf sagging in the slime. The putrid odor of stagnant water assailed him.

The writer is trying too hard. In prose as in painting, it is impossible to put every leaf on the tree; a few of them may safely be left to the reader's imagination. The diction appropriate to a particular story depends upon the kind of story, upon the kind of reader, but the "lean, terse style" is one towards which most beginners can profitably struggle. Even when, after a revision or two, some of the repetitions and ornamentations are put back into paragraphs earlier denuded of them, the practice of deciding upon their removal, upon their retention, is practice of the best.

1. It was quite by accident that Ada North happened to buy that particular book. It wasn't the sort of thing she was in the habit of reading. She never was sure what obscure impulse within her prompted her to do such a thing. But she *did* buy the book, and it was responsible for the whole thing.

It all started upon a very stormy Saturday afternoon soon after lunch. She had gone back to the office to finish up some important details for Mr. Grigsby. She really could have let those papers go until Monday, but Ada was an exceptionally efficient secretary who believed implicitly in the motto, "Never put off until tomorrow what you can do today." She often told the younger girls in the office that that was one of the important maxims of a good secretary. If she had not returned to the office, she would not have received Homer's message until she had gone home; and so, of course, she would never have bought that book.

2. As Claire dressed, she pictured in her mind the entrance she would make when Philip came. It was seven-thirty, and he would arrive for eight o'clock dinner. She could make a very nice entrance if she could go down the stairway—sort of glide down— with him at the bottom, looking up, waiting for her. That would be rather graceful. But then again, it would probably be more convenient if she just let Etta take him into the library when he came. She might not be ready by the time he arrived. And then he could talk to Father until she came downstairs.

3. All of the increasing group centered around the drowned boy, who was laid on blankets on the sand. The other fishermen started working on him, while the woman had to be wrenched from her son by the two men who had accompanied her. Insufferable minutes ensued. He seemed most certainly dead, responding to no treatment. But no, his eyelids moved. No, it was just an accident. Yes, he was alive.

Everyone was excited. People pressed closer. Yes, he seemed all right now. He was breathing regularly and already a little warmth returned to his body. All he needed now was plenty of rest and he ought to pull through. Some one seemed to be taking the initiative. Matters were taking on a more commonplace air, so that gradually the crowd began to drop away.

In each of the three passages above, count the number of restatements not of word but of idea. In the opening paragraph of the first one, Ada North happens to buy a book, does not usually buy that kind of book, is not sure why she buys it, but—climax of the paragraph—does buy it. The second paragraph is as bad, stating and restating the fact of Ada's meticulousness. These restatements are not the repetitions meant to drive home to a reader's mind the various importances of a story. They are no more than the unwinding into words of a heavy and unilluminated mind. In the first and third passages especially, note the mind's attempt to escape from labor by retreat into loose and general terms— ". . . the whole thing. It all started. . . . Some one seemed to be taking the initiative. Matters were taking on a commonplace air." Even without the fold on fold of restatement, this is wording murderous to reader's interest.

Oliver Kendrick stood listlessly by the windows. He eyed the dull sandstone building across the street, looking uninterestedly at the white-coated dentist dimly visible behind a smudged gilt sign. Far up, a drab brown figure hung precariously by slender straps, one hand clutching a heavy bucket and the other busily scouring a dirty window pane. Below him, the frowsy head of a stenographer rose and fell, rose and fell, in little, uneasy jerks as she bent and straightened over her machine. A film of dirty cloud bridged the space between the buildings.

The paragraph is the opening for a story of disillusionment and ruin. In the story, Oliver is considering suicide, and suicide by the inconsiderate method of hurtling from his window down to the street below. He is entitled, therefore, to turn upon the scene in front of him a jaundiced eye. Dreary and repulsive that street would undoubtedly look to Oliver. His maker's theory, then, is this: Whatever meets Oliver's gaze will take the color of the eye regarding it. Let him look out on the street. Set down one thing he sees, another, still another. When you have set down enough, each tinged by Oliver's somber view, the cumulative effect will produce in a reader some part of Oliver's emotion. It will—unless, long before that emotion is produced, the reader has revolted and produced an emotion of his own towards the whole story.

The "look-by-look" method of writing which Oliver illustrates does occasionally do exactly what it is intended to do, but it is a method easy to over-use and especially in opening paragraphs. Intense emotion lies always close to absurdity. Insistence on emotion at the beginning of a story, multiplying and remultiplying of details meant to produce it, is work for a practiced hand. Between being appalled at Oliver's plight and being amused at the author's attempt to appall you, the distance is perilously short.

The overburdening of the passages shown thus far has come, in general, from the writer's fear that he will not hold readers' attention long enough to produce the effect he wants. A struggle for effect harder to define, much harder to alter, is that which shows itself in precious writing.

At what point writing becomes precious, how much ornament a given style, a given subject, can carry, is a thing individually to be decided, and less from story to story than from writer to writer. A powerful mind, a sweep of feeling, a wide experience deeply pondered—these things make possible to their possessor use of images and special adaptations of words which a meaner endowment may not risk. But for most stories and most writers, deliberate ornamentation needs much scrutiny before it is allowed a place in finished work. Phrases pushing up like mushrooms above the level of the narrative have a habit of turning out to be toadstools. "Take out whatever you particularly like" is hard counsel, but oftener than not it is wise counsel as well.

To me, the new store appeared as a plate-glass, cellophane-wrapped, linoleumed palace.

The life in her was guarded from anguish by a china fine body, and she always wore pale chiffon in the evening, palest pink and blue and lavender. Tonight she was wearing lavender and her vital fire was burning high.

He came from nowhere and from everywhere—a wandering man with his violin. About him the lure of far places; in his strange, dark eyes too much knowledge, perhaps of love. And it was spring when he came to the village.

A ladder of moonbeams reached to the couch, the light of its beauty revealing the incongruity of one slippered and one nude foot.

Preciousness in each of these passages drops to prettifying, to a wearying struggle for originality disadvantageous to both reader and writer. On the reader's side, the wording distracts him from what the writer is trying to say; a story is not made up of a phrase plus a phrase any more than it is made up of an incident plus an incident. On the writer's side, excessive care for the pictorial quality of words, continual conscious struggle for the striking phrase, results often in loss of spontaneity. A piddling habit grows from story to story till at last idea is habitually subordinated to expression. For the excerpts shown here, cutting and the substitution of phrases less tortured and elaborated will redeem them. For their writers, there is redemption only through a patient study of the values of simplicity. With every beginner at writing, the attempt to make sentences say exactly what he means comes far in advance of the attempt to make them say it with elaboration.

Simplicity, however, is not identical with commonplaceness. Preciousness pushes language above the level of the emotion or information it has to carry. Wording actually commonplace falls below the emotional level of its substance, is vague, inaccurate, shopworn.

"Isn't it quiet?" The whispered question gave the guide quite a start.

The guide is planning to murder the whisperer. That "quite a start" makes farcical both his feeling and the laboriously manufactured situation.

She was sort of afraid he would come after her, and she did not know what she would do if he did.
It seemed to her he must be badly hurt, so she began to cry and scream.

Unlike preciousness, the elimination of commonplaceness in diction is not to be accomplished by the reworking of particular passages. What does accomplish it, and then only gradually, is the development, through reading and listening, of a sensitiveness to the effect of words.

He felt he had to leave, though doings at the party were just well under way.

Here is commonplaceness again but commonplaceness of a different kind. Only a reader of abnormally lively imagination can translate "doings at the party" into visual image. The writer's failure to make the translation himself was probably the reason for his phrasing. No rule is safe to follow always, but the rule that presentations in a story should be specific comes as near to being always a safe guide as any rule can.

"Dr. Anderson was well dressed" gives the reader next to nothing; "Dr. Anderson buttoned his expensive tweed coat . . ." There is material for making a picture. "The way she was dressed made her look cool even in all the heat." "She was in white from neck to shoes." "He made as much noise inside the room as he could, trying to attract the other man's attention." "He shouted, 'Bill! Bill!' at the top of his lungs, and beat his fists against the door."

Failure to particularize is most often the result of mental laziness. Mental laziness accounts, too, for the borrowing habit conspicuous among dealers in the commonplace. "Came the dawn" has at last been laughed out of existence, but successors to it appear, each a burr stuck to the manuscript of some writer who longs for originality but is unable to produce it. Any writer may be sure that a striking phrase, a striking word arrangement, fathered by someone else has not met his eyes alone. It will reappear in his story and in enough others to make it presently anathema to readers.

Borrowing other people's phrases is a practice easily recognized and easily discontinued. Less easy to discontinue is the habit of letting your own chosen words tell something other than the truth. "Willows whiten, aspens quiver," wrote Tennyson a couple of generations ago, and made visible for the first time to a million readers the changing color of a willow's leaves when the wind turns them. "The live oaks quivering and shuddering outside her window" wrote a less scrupulous observer of the most stable, the most unquivering, of trees. Observation is cultivatable; where cultivation has not yet gone far, it is worth while to verify statements before they reach their final place on the page.

Whenever the conversation turned to the beauties of the world, Mary would say to her friends, "I never could see anything so marvelous about nature. I've sat and positively stared . . ."

Mary's maker is not intentionally assigning to her a role more repetitive than that of the Three Bears. He has done no more than fail to understand the effect upon a sentence of *whenever* and *would,* and so has said what he had no purpose in saying. Guesswork presentation of material supposedly factual, stating of the specific as though it were the general —these two things account for perhaps half the verbal untruths which find their way into stories.

The other half is accounted for by the slipshod use of individual words. The writer who speaks of quivering live oaks may defend his choice of adjective or may plead imperfect noticing. The writer who permits the teller of his story to say, "There was something in his manner which seemed to inflame me," has no shield for his incompetence. Neither has the writer who announces his hero as "dull and disinterested because of the heat." A dictionary is indispensable on any beginner's shelf. A handbook on English composition may well sit beside it. Neither is an infallible guide, but both assist in keeping sharp the edges of meaning, the finer points of usage. And for a writer, to use words truthfully is quite as important as to tell the truth with the ones he uses.

Against one propensity of words, and especially of English words, every writer has to be on guard. This is their propensity for picking up additional meanings, slang or otherwise, which crowd the accepted meaning off the page. Ford Madox Ford, in *Joseph Conrad, a Remembrance,* records

Conrad's indictment of the English language, ". . . that no English word is a word; that all English words are instruments for exciting blurred emotions . . . no English word has clean edges." He uses the word "oaken" as an example, a word which, in French, means "made of oak" and nothing more. In English, "heart of oak," "oaken strength," and the like do not refer to actual oak at all but instead connote moral qualities.

Against these attached meanings, all a writer can do is to keep his ears sensitive to contemporary usage and to make the surroundings of his word such that the intended meaning is inevitable. "She flew to meet her lover." Did she hurry or did she take passage in an airplane?

III

Seeing her standing smiling there, he stopped, smiling himself at her gracious unspoken greeting.

The hissing and grinding sentence above was constructed by a usually careful writer and was published in a reputable magazine. It is reproduced here as exemplification of a truth every writer comes early to know. Reading over his manuscript, he will pass by sentences which later, seen in print, set his teeth on edge. Stevenson speaks of finding himself "riding the flat *a*" through the length of a page. Sometimes it is the flat *a;* sometimes, as in the sentence above, it is *s* and *g*. Sometimes it is not a sound but a phrase. There are passages in Chesterton's essays in which the qualifying *A certain* —"A certain pleasure . . . a certain doubt . . . a certain

reservation . . . a certain author"—comes to affect the
reader as the modifier "good ole," tacked to every noun, affected Penrod Scofield's companions.

Or instead of a single phrase, it may be a flock of one-syl-
lable words, or a flock of two-syllable ones, word accents and
sense accents falling at different points. Sometimes it is a
series of sentences made all to the same monotonous measure.
In third-person telling always, and usually in first-person
telling as well, repeated use destroys the effectiveness of any
sentence form. If a writer's ear does not make that announcement to him, then he must either give up fiction or slowly
cultivate the capacity for hearing sentence rhythms.

Ugliness in writing is limited to no one kind. And just as
there is no one ugliness, there is no one cure. The nearest to
a general panacea is the beginner's persistent reading aloud
of his work, reading it softly, without listeners and without
oratory; reading it, if he can, as intently, as dispassionately,
as a doctor fingers down the vertebræ of the spine in search
of injury.

But reading his own work aloud can improve it only up to
the level of the reader's taste. For raising that level, there is
no substitute for the reading of other people's prose and
good prose at that.

What "good" consists of is, of course, capable of no final
definition; a working definition, however, is easy to reach.
For a given writer at any given moment, good prose is that
which he recognizes as better than his own, that which
awakens admiration and which he reads and rereads for the
love of reading it. What it will be nobody can tell. Nobody
can tell, either, how many times his taste may change, trans-
forming what once was stirring into bombast, what once was

touching into bathos. It is a safe guess, though, that he will be correct in believing the prose which delights him at the moment to be better than the prose he writes. If he can find it, if he can read it in solitude, trying over a sentence aloud, picking out a phrase, vocalizing it, repeating it, ringing it in the air, he is doing as much as can be done for his own improvement. If he can do it not for the sake of improvement but out of sheer love, his case is better still, for not many people are capable of writing who are incapable of a single-minded delight in the sound of words.

Analysis of effective phrases is not in question here. What is in question is only the recognition of their qualities. Probably nobody ever learned to write whose recognitions were not instinctive rather than reasoned. Analysis of ugly phrases, on the other hand, does have a limited value. In the passages considered in the earlier sections of this chapter, it was evident that not all of the ugliness of ugly sentences came from the words alone. Much of it came from the relationships between words. Change the order in some familiar line, and this truth is instantly exemplified.

"Time like a many-colored dome of glass . . ."

"Time like a dome of many-colored glass . . ."

Nobody with an ounce of writing feeling can doubt which line the poet wrote. And in prose, the placing of words is no less important than in verse. Certain principles concerning this placing are taught most children in grade school. Many adults, however, need to relearn them.

One of these principles is that you cannot alter the normal word order of English sentences without paying for your alterations. What is that normal order? Let us look at a few decent but undistinguished sentences and see.

The dark, cloudy sky promised rain.

A handsome, sullen boy stood beside me, waiting for the storm to cease.

Mary walked into the classroom and sat down in a last row seat in order to have a good view of the other students as they arrived.

In all three, we have the accustomed form of English speech and of English writing—the one from which the exceptions, though frequent, remain exceptions still.

The sky, dark, cloudy, promised rain.

Beside me, waiting for the storm to cease, stood a boy, handsome, sullen.

It is apparent to any reader that the sky has become more threatening, the boy's sullenness been increased by the change in word order. As for Mary and her last row seat— but Mary is left for the reader's rearrangement. What is evident from the first two sentences is this: Give to a word an unusual place in a sentence and you give it thereby an added emphasis, an added importance.

And I remembered how, long ago, I had paused and wondered on that same bridge.

Return the "long ago" to the end of the sentence. You have shortened the elapsed time by years.

When, therefore, a writer pushes a word out of its place,

he does so, if he is wise, because that word is of special note, not because he is erratically trying for originality. If the word is not of an importance equal to its special placing, what he accomplishes is the confusion of his readers and the further confusion of his own sense of word values.

There are other grade-school precepts useful to remember: that words connected in thought should, as often as possible, be kept together in a sentence; that the beginnings and the ends of sentences, the beginnings and the ends of paragraphs, offer placings of unusual prominence. Ugly passages, tested against these simplicities, may lose their conspicuous ugliness. For any advance beyond the loss of ugliness, word placing must be done by ear. That "unremitting, never discouraged care for the shape and ring of sentences" advised by Joseph Conrad is the necessity of every writer—of every writer who means to be more than a hack.

Trying the sentences over, then, in the story you are now at work on, is their tune right? Trying them in little groups, seldom more than a page at a time, do they have the ring you want? If they do not, is it because of wordiness, of preciousness, of commonplaceness, of arrangement?

Of the sentences below, so far as a sentence can be judged apart from its context, which were written by skilled and which by unskilled hands? And what in the sentence influences your judgment?

1. Brick by brick he had built it himself, working evenings and Sundays.

2. For a solid hour he had been contemplating imminent death.

3. Her long face was innocent, indeed ignorant, of cosmetics.

4. In fact, once thought of, the thought needed little verification, for, as Clarice realized, it was exactly what any person with a trace of exhibitionism in his make-up—and all of us have the trace—would do.

5. It must have taken me, for my broken, difficult account, half an hour.

6. After a while I said, "I'm sorry that I won't be here to see her, but we're leaving tomorrow and probably we won't be back until Christmas."

7. Tufts of golden hair peeked out from below her trim little hat.

8. "Listen—" Both men stiffened automatically; the sailor at the wheel, tightening his grasp on the spokes nervously, watched the officers anxiously.

9. It was not as deep as it had looked nor as he had feared it was.

IV

Discussion of revision so far has dealt with revision within the sentence. A watchful rereading of the finished story is needed too for discovery of omissions of necessary information, another in search of incongruities or misleading implications. To find what facts are wanting, a beginner's safest plan is to formulate a series of questions about his story, then search the opening pages for answers. The rule known to all would-be reporters—time, place, person made clear in the opening lines—is one only an experienced writer can afford to disregard, and an experienced writer rarely does. Beyond "time, place, person," however, information has to be slid in largely by feel. A necessary fact must be located at one point, re-located at another, till an unobtrusive placing is found for it. Consider, for example, the placings in the following paragraphs.

Tea was being served in the garden. Joan enjoyed tea in the garden, yet this afternoon she paused discomfited on the verandah steps, regretting that she had come out so thoughtlessly. There were guests about the table under the willow, and Joan was immediately conscious of the contrast between her dark blue dress and the delicately shaded ones of those gathered in the garden. Why had she not stopped to change after coming down from delving amongst those old books up in the attic? Well, she had been seen by this time; she would just explain, though it would probably be thought an extremely odd thing for a young woman to be doing on a hot summer afternoon. She advanced across the lawn to meet the distressed glance of her mother. The men arose; there were mild greetings to which Joan quietly responded, adding at the conclusion, "Pray pardon my dull appearance; I have been up in the attic looking through some old books of grandfather's, and did not realize . . ."

"You look most charming as you are, my dear. If you followed my advice you would wear darker colors all the time." Old Colonel Craddock always came to her rescue. He was interrupted by Mrs. Hatburn.

"Yes, I think blue is really a most cool color. Mrs. Fairfax wore such a beautiful gown of Alice blue at the Curtis ball last week. . . ." Several of the other ladies chimed in with ecstatic comments, and the conversation turned from Joan to the fertile field of fashion.

The story which is to follow has for its time setting the years immediately after the Civil War. Its time setting is important, for Joan's revolt against the mid-Victorian expectations of her family is what the story is about, and yet any reader might finish not only the opening paragraphs but the opening pages without knowing when the action took place.

In the paragraphs given, where can opportunity be found for stating what is now only vaguely suggested? And what chances has the writer overlooked for reinforcing statement by use of descriptive details?

And now, at the end of the chapter, a question: How much of this labor of revision does a writer really need to do? How much of it can he get along without? . . . Well, a great deal. If he has gusto, inventiveness, keen observation, then he may use individual words, form individual sentences, clumsily, verbosely, and still win readers. It is a question of amount, of what his whole store of abilities adds up to. One ability, any one, can be spared if the rest make a sufficient total. But there are abilities which are born, not made. No man by taking thought can add to his native gusto; to his native inventiveness he can add only in the smallest degree. Words, on the other hand, can be dealt with. By sufficient care, he can at times "bring the light of magic suggestiveness . . . to play over the commonplace surface of the old, old words."

Nor is the reason for struggling toward that "magic suggestiveness" one connected with publication only. A writer writes for readers but not for readers solely. Writing is lonely work, hard work, nerve straining. It is still lonelier, still harder, far more nerve straining if the writer is not also a craftsman. Unless he actually enjoys his craft, enjoys the labor of it, respects the materials he works with, any prospective writer should thoroughly examine his purpose before the struggle to subdue words is begun. Does he want to write? Or does he want only to have written? There is a notable difference.

X

Conclusion

1. Forming Writing Habits.
2. Placing Stories.

Conclusion

1. Forming Writing Habits

ANY substantial increase in writing ability arrives as a re-sult of general growth plus writing practice, and arrives only so. What experiences promote growth and what devices en-hance the usefulness of practice are, in large measure, mat-ters of individual decision. Nonetheless, there are certain ways of dealing with experience which are profitable to con-sider and certain hindrances to successful practice against which a beginner can be forewarned.

First, for experience: All but invariably a story gets its earliest impulse from some nub of fact. All but invariably, too, the finished story rests not on that one nub but on many. Lord Peter Wimsey rescues the Medway diamonds because he is conscious of the difference between the feminine and the masculine form of a French noun. John Russell brings his boatman safe through danger because Russell knows the construction of a coracle. Lacking its special bit of central knowledge, neither story could have reached its conclusion. Presumably neither could have been conceived, not because the required information could not have been hunted out when required, but because no story would come to mind unless the fact was there in advance. Fact, that is, is the springboard of the imagination. All the way from exotic to familiar, from large to small, it is a writer's most necessary possession—his most necessary except one, and that is the inflammable imagination to which the fact applies the spark.

Imagination, however, is mostly a gift of God; facts can be acquired. And it is not only at the crisis of a story but at every stage, almost with every paragraph, that some bit of exact knowledge helps the narrative forward. Maugham's recollection of the Freudian interpretation of a given dream does not affect the tragic action of *Rain;* what it does do is help to convince the reader of the validity of that action. *A Worn Path,* by Eudora Welty, a story as delicate as this-tledown, yet demands a knowledge of seasonal growths and hunting seasons, of the processes of a free clinic. Jessamyn West rests *The Friendly Persuasion* on her knowledge of Quaker ways and Quaker speech, but a considerable portion of orchardist's lore is caught up in the stories too. Few need to be reminded that information profuse and minute concerning tractors—their construction, their performance, their marketing—is the oak-solid stage on which Alexander Botts plays out his comedies.

Of Lord Peter Wimsey, his maker tells us that his conduct "was regulated—by a persistent and undignified inquisitiveness" and that some of the results of that inquisitiveness were entombed in "a bulky manuscript—biographies of the most unexpected people, and the most unexpected facts about the most obvious people." Lord Peter is a specialist, but quite apart from his specialty, this imaginary activity of an imaginary detective is worth consideration. Unending inquisitiveness, unending patience in verifying and recording the material turned up by that inquisitiveness—a better prescription for fiction planning could hardly be provided. One ingredient only is lacking, and that one is found in the third chapter of John Livingston Lowes' *The Road to Xanadu* (the chapter called "The Deep Well"), too long for quoting but good for many readings.

Some factual material the daily drift of life brings with it always, but the daily drift, unaided, rarely brings enough and tends ordinarily to bring less with the passing of each decade. A writer who means to keep on writing needs consciously to add to his store. Otherwise, as several lamentable present-day examples go to show, he falls into writing the same story over and over in slightly altered guises and worse each time till either he passes out of print or is kept there only by his noisy adherence to some *ism* which brings him his patient special readers. What kind of facts are to be added does not make much difference except as concerns size of audience attracted. Some audience there is for any variety. Baseball, tractor selling, criminal law, cookery, the collection of period furniture—each of these has served recently for stories and for series of stories. Whatever stimulates the individual imagination, whatever the writer likes to collect is likely to stand him in good stead. Many times, of course, the "fact" which does stimulate imagination is fact by courtesy only. Does a snake actually return to kill the killer of its mate? Can hypnotic influence be despatched from orchestra seat to stage? Is it conceivable that invisible animals exist which can kill and mangle their victims? All that can be said is that these "facts" and dozens like them have set stories on their way.

No one kind of research and collection, then, is necessarily more provocative of the writing feeling than any other kind. What is necessary is that fact collecting in whatever field should go far enough to carry the collector beyond what is known to almost everybody and should be accurate enough not to disillusion readers who have some knowledge. Naturally, it ought also to interest the collector intensely if its results, seeping out on paper, are to arouse interest in other people. And any exact knowledge is the more likely to be useful if its possessor, like Lord Peter, embeds it in written record. Many of the things which go into a notebook—plots especially—are oftener entombed than embedded; facts are the exception.

For the beginner at writing, the requirements just stated present an obvious dilemma. Most beginners must earn their livings by means other than writing; all must have frequent writing practice. Between the two "must's," life is in danger of becoming a treadmill—so many hours for business, so many for coming and going, so many for food, so many for struggling with words, deadened sleep to follow. No time is left for pushing knowledge of anything beyond its earliest borders, no time for reading, day-dreaming, recreation—all of them essential feeders to talent. How is a beginner to lay hold of these essentials? The only answer is that somehow some beginners do; that those who do, learn to conserve their time, to pay it out only for profitable ends, and especially to increase the productivity of such writing hours as they can get.

At this last point is where devices come in. And they are exactly what their name denotes—not methods but merely tricks, ways of catching the mind halfway unawares and putting it into harness. Before any device can be put to use, however, the beginner has to free himself from two fallacies common to nearly all his kind. One of these is that his over-busy state is transient, that next year, next month, next week will be freer than the present one from interruptions. Next year, next week never is. Time for writing continually recedes into the distance except as planning and ruthless eliminations make space for it. Another fallacy is to suppose that smallness of production has somehow a relation to excellence. Amount—or, rather, scantiness—of work brought forth in any given day or month is, of course, no criterion, but the novice who sits week following week in front of his dog-eared sheets, adding next to nothing to their content, is probably self-deceived if he believes the quality of his work accounts for its lack of quantity. Writing skill comes from writing, not from intending to write. What is written may deserve only to be torn up, but the act of writing is essential. Till these certitudes are set in mind, no devices will help.

A first device for the protection of writing time and so for the improvement of output is the obtaining of relatively favorable surroundings for such working hours as the writer has. It is not a self-indulgence, a symptom of over-developed ego, to ward off interruptions, for though it is possible to write between interruptions, just as it is possible for some persons to write in the midst of tumult, ordinarily the same amount of effort produces a better result when interruption and tumult are eliminated. Ordinarily too a special time for writing, a special place, are worth what it costs to achieve them. They are worth it because each aids, even if only a little, in surmounting the chief stumbling block of all. This is the slow arrival of the writing feeling—two hours or three set aside for writing and half the time gone before the mind comes under control. Will power brings it under at last, but whatever can be saved by regulation of externals is so much clear gain.

And usually a good deal can be saved. Even apart from relative quiet, from regular writing hours and writing place, nearly every person can also help himself by special aids. To find out early what these aids are—the special ones that are aids to you—to see that they are at hand, is to shorten apprenticeship. What you are trying for is a release of the mind from thoughts of the day's work, a quickening of it for new and different effort. One writer, not unsuccessful, has a favorite record which he plays over, sometimes over and over, while he is settling to work. Another, luckily located, tramps through meadows for half an hour as prelude to his three hours of very early morning writing. Means are less numerous than writers, but even so, there are many of them. A crystal ball on the table; a transparency in the window, holding the eyes with its patch of blue or scarlet; the murmuring over of verse—these and others serve to give the mind a lift from weariness.

2. Placing Stories

There are three ways of placing stories. The first and alluring way is, of course, to sell them. The second is to dispose of them to some Little Magazine which offers publication and possibly prestige but no pay. The third is to stow them in trunks or bottom bureau drawers, leaving them there against the time of the writer's further ripening. Ordinarily, a beginner tries these three ways in the order here named. This present very brief discussion purposes to consider them in inverse order.

A good deal is to be said in behalf of the trunk and the bureau drawer. Somerset Maugham speaks, in *The Summing Up,* of having been kept by a blessed misfortune from exploiting a subject before he knew how to handle it. Many writers less eminent have had the same experience. Though their creators, naturally, do not see them so, early writing efforts are more likely to be exercises than stories. For an exercise, the suitable refuge is a storage place from which it may be drawn from time to time for contrast with the writer's later work.

A Little Magazine, one depending for its existence on unpaid or barely paid contributors, may provide important helps. It offers the writer a chance to see how his work looks in print, frequently a chance for critical comment from outside his own circle, and now and then the high encouragement of having his stories noticed in places other than that of their first appearance. Against these advantages, however, are set several possible hindrances. These spring from the Little Magazines' staffs and supporters being not infrequently grievance groups, people convinced that congeries of writers more widely recognized than their own are necessarily inferior; or else, as frequently, they are supporters of some literary *ism* which renders them incapable of distinguishing better from worse except as "better" wears their particular label. Those Little Magazines devoted to regional interests are more likely, apparently, than their fellows to escape this curse of over-righteousness, since they possess a reason for existence other than scorn of their contemporaries. Some of the rest escape too, but so swiftly do most of them appear and disappear that which these are each person has to decide for himself. The decision is important, for any periodical which welcomes a beginner's work is certain to exercise on him a strong influence, one finally advantageous or finally stultifying. And in all his first years of practice, growth is more important to the writer than is early publication.

Trying to publish, however, even from the first awkward endeavor, has harm in it only insofar as the person trying allows the effort to waste his time or distract his attention, or as it piles up in him a sense of grievance. This last is a danger not to be minimized. There is no town, there is scarcely a flag station, which does not number among its inhabitants some prolific but unpublished writer ready to point out in any issue of any magazine stories inferior, in his own eyes, to the ones he impatiently mails and re-mails, and indignantly certain therefore that worth in fiction is overlooked in favor of distinguished names. In some very small measure, too, he is justified. Distinguished names do incline editors to acceptance. They do because they also incline readers to reading. A reader prefers to know something of the writer to whom he surrenders his time just as a patient wishes to know something of the surgeon to whom he surrenders his appendix. Any other attitude would be unreasonable in editor and reader alike.

Equally unreasonable and equally frequent is the attitude of the disappointed struggler with fiction who feels that because he ardently wants his work to be published, somebody should want to publish it. The unreasonableness is worth mention because attitude of mind is what writing springs from. The self-centered, the self-pitying, the grudge-bearing attitude is that much more weight to carry against competitors less burdened.

And the weight is carried unnecessarily. Stories of substance, stories well planned and well written, which yet fail to be published probably do exist. They are rarer, though, than white blackbirds. When a would-be writer has pursued his craft through a three- or four-year apprenticeship and has at last produced a really good story, he can supply himself with stamps and envelopes in a mood of entire tranquility. His really good story may not stay with the first editor who sees it nor even with the second, but it will stay somewhere.

For the saving of his time, he will do well to make out, in advance of sending out what he thinks is a salable story, a list of magazines, beginning with those he would most like, but does not really hope, to attain. The manuscript returning from one editor, he starts it immediately towards another. Whether he sends it out himself or finds an agent to send it for him, whether the pages are dog-eared or immaculate, its final success will be about the same. If there is suspense or mirth or pathos in it, it will not reach the end of his list.

Appendix

I

Minnie

MINNIE was born and brought up in Raeder. If you think you know a worse fate, produce it for comparison.

Her mother, whose relation to the Caesar ladies was tolerably distant, dispensed with her husband about the time that Minnie was learning to creep. Later, she married another husband and dispensed with him, and later still eschewed matrimony and took to restaurant keeping.

Minnie took her infant naps in a clothesbasket under the long restaurant counter. She shed her infant teeth in vain attempts on "steak-'r-chops," dressed up T-bones for dolls, and fought with cats outside the back entrance for the safety of her creations.

About the time she was able to outwit the cats, she became old enough simultaneously for school and dishwashing. After that, she was a factor in economic conditions. Raeder has something less than a thousand inhabitants, each of whom knows or knows about all the rest. No teacher was ever so unreasonable as to expect excellence of "that Gans girl," and no teacher ever got from her more than she expected. Dishwashing, on the other hand, might fairly be called a gift by inheritance. She prospered exceedingly at it. She added a rough and ready knowledge of cookery almost by instinct, and that capacity for scrubbing without the removal of dirt which is a near approach to genius. By the time she was sixteen, she could carry five full meals deftly balanced between wrist and shoulder, she could serve up short orders with the maximum of speed, and she had developed an admiration for her mother which was almost a passion.

1. The four paragraphs above cover sixteen years of time. What are the phrases by means of which the writer keeps the reader aware of time's passage?

2. What excerpt quoted in *Time* uses a similar method?

3. ". . . with every story, he, the writer, faces the question of how to crowd into his first paragraphs an extra ten years or so of his person's experience." What are some of the devices by which the author of "Minnie" fits in needed information?

4. Rewrite the passage, using minute-to-minute treatment but keeping the rewritten account within the space now allowed it. What means can you find for so keeping it?

5. What is the point of observation from which "Minnie" is written? Note the sentences which prove your assertion to be right.

6. In *Points of Observation,* p. 88, are listed the ways in which the story of X, Y, and Mrs. Y may be told. So far as the paragraphs given show, which of these ways are precluded by the material of this story?

7. "Her mother, who was a woman of doubtful character, was separated from her husband when Minnie was eight months old." Contrast this sentence with the original. The two are identical in sense. What does the original sentence do which this one does not?

8. What is the value of the word "tolerably" where it now stands?

9. Pick three words other than "tolerably" which make large contribution to the tone of the excerpt as well as to its meaning.

10. What tone does the excerpt have?

11. Rewrite one paragraph, giving it another tone consistently sustained.

Mr. Simms

Mr. Simms reached over the side of his bed and turned off the alarm clock with a grunt of displeasure. He did not feel rested. He wanted to sleep a few more hours yet; he knew he'd have a bad day if he arose feeling tired. But he must face facts; a business man can afford himself no dilly-dallying about in bed in the morning. It was seven o'clock. He must get up. He arose and walked over to the window which looked out upon a gray and cheerless morning fog. Another drizzly day, he remarked to himself. A pity that the sun never shone in San Francisco.

He arrived at the breakfast table four minutes earlier than usual. Mr. Simms always kept track of the time, all day long. It made one's day more organized, somehow. He liked to keep track of the minutes as he dressed in the morning, as he ate his breakfast, his lunch, and his dinner. There was no time for minute-wasting in the world of business!

Adjusting the pince-nez on the high bony ridge of his nose, Mr. Simms snorted mildly at the scrambled eggs before him. Too moist; hadn't he told her a hundred times in the last five years that he couldn't eat them when they were too moist! And the toast! But Mr. Simms did not like to complain of things when Sarah looked cross. For then she would fly into a rage, refuse to finish whatever she was doing, and declare wrathfully that she would leave and find some place else to work. He remembered this particular speech of hers. It was the same every time, but she had never left. She had, in fact, threatened to leave only three or four times during the past five years. It would be unpleasant if she did ever get it into her head to go. It would be unpleasant getting used to having someone new around. There was something rather comfortable and familiar about having the same person there every day. Sarah's extravagantly plump figure and her old, rather tired face was a part of Mr. Simms' order of things. Without her, his routine would be entirely disrupted.

1. The paragraphs quoted form the opening of a story dealing with one day in Mr. Simms' life. As it is now written, the passage contains 370 words. Bring it down to 200 without loss of substance or change in the presentation of Mr. Simms.

2. If you could delete one word and only one from each paragraph of the original passage, which word would it be?

3. From "Adjusting the pince-nez" to "past five years," read the sentences aloud and formulate advice to the writer about sentence making.

4. What kind of person is Mr. Simms shown to be?

5. What are the phrases which characterize him?

6. Is the characterization one which arouses interest? If it does not, is it by reason of Mr. Simms' being intrinsically uninteresting or by reason of the way he is presented?

7. Is it possible to write an interesting story in which the main figure is personally uninteresting? Support your answer by evidence drawn from your own reading or writing.

8. Can you call to mind some person you know who is consistently dull? So far as your acquaintance with the person allows, record the evidences of dullness and analyze their probable causes.

9. Write a brief sketch of a dull person, showing that the person is dull but making the sketch interesting.

10. ". . . what is to make an impression on a reader must be repeated and re-repeated, ground into his mind by repetition." Beginning with the phrase, "Mr. Simms did not like to complain," count the repetitions of idea in the rest of the paragraph. Since repetition itself is necessary, what makes these repetitions ineffective?

Mrs. Haines

Mrs. Julia Haines, long and lean and blanket-swathed, sat on a bench outside her son-in-law's ranch-house door. It was the tenth week of her ranch residence, and her fifth day of escape from bed.

Inside the house her daughter Mattie, ten weeks a wife, glanced out anxiously now and then in the intervals of her dishwashing. She had not approved of the expedition out of doors, but she had not known how to prevent it. Mattie was not quite seventeen. For sixteen years and six months of her life she had lived and breathed and had her being in strict obedience to her mother's will. The external reasons for that obedience were gone now, but the habit of it remained.

"An' yet I got to take care of her," the daughter admonished herself. "Whether she likes it or not, I got to. Till she gets good an' strong, anyhow."

She tiptoed to the window and looked out. Mrs. Haines sat crumpled upon her bench, her head thrown back, her sallow eyelids drawn close against the sun.

"Asleep," Mattie diagnosed the attitude with satisfaction and went back to her pans.

"Thinks I'm asleep," the invalid interpreted, listening to the retreating footsteps. So deep within her that the haggard mask of face was undisturbed, she was smiling over the misapprehension. Mattie in the role of caretaker filled her mother with satiric mirth.

"Though it was time she growed up," the listener admitted. "I kep' her back long enough. An' she's got a good man."

1. What is the point of observation from which "Mrs. Haines" is written?

2. What advantage, if any, do you see in the writer's having chosen this point?

3. Rewrite the paragraphs given, leaving out none of the information to the reader now included but allowing yourself entrance into only one of the two minds.

4. What influenced you to choose one mind rather than the other?

5. Does the writer, in this first page of his story, show you which of the two characters is to be the more interesting? What attributes are assigned to her to make her the more interesting?

6. In what phrases does the writer show you the social status of the two persons in his story? Their economic status?

7. Where, if at all, do these opening paragraphs suggest the general idea which is to hold the incidents together?

8. Approximately how much time does this opening page actually show? How much does it account for?

1. The beginnings of three stories have been given above. Which one should you least unwillingly continue reading?

2. Does any one of the three repel you? What causes it to be repellent?

3. Of these stories, which comes nearest to making clear time, place, person, circumstance in its opening paragraphs?

4. Summarize in a sentence your impression of one of the characters shown.

5. Character, personified trait, and caricature are all possible in the presentation of persons in a story. Place each of the persons shown in these beginnings in its proper category.

II

A

All round the circle of the hills the dazzling sky pressed down unclouded to the touch of the parched rimrock. Between the hills, the shallow basin lay baked and breathless.

Over it the tense air quivered with heat. Within, no bird fluttered, no water purled, no green plant raised its head. Only the desert children, sagebrush and greasewood and long-spined cactus, gray but never dying, lived on there in the drought, sterile and forbidding as the land which gave them birth. Everywhere was silence upon the place, everywhere was immobility.

There are hills, rounded, blunt, burned, squeezed up out of chaos, chrome and vermilion painted, aspiring to the snow line. Between the hills lie high level-looking plains full of intolerable sun glare, or narrow valleys drowned in a blue haze. The hill surface is streaked with ash drift and black, unweathered lava flows. After rains water accumulates in the hollows of small closed valleys, and, evaporating, leaves hard dry levels of pure desertness that get the local name of dry lakes. Where the mountains are steep and the rains heavy, the pool is never quite dry, but dark and bitter, rimmed about with the efflorescence of alkaline deposits. A thin crust of it lies along the marsh over the vegetating area, which has neither beauty nor freshness. In the broad wastes open to the wind the sand drifts in hummocks about the stubby shrubs, and between them the soil shows saline traces. The sculpture of the hills here is more wind than water work, though the quick storms do sometimes scar them past many a year's redeeming. In all the Western desert edges there are essays in miniature at the famed, terrible Grand Canyon, to which, if you keep on long enough in this country, you will come at last.

—Mary Austin. *The Land of Little Rain.**

* Excerpt used by permission of Houghton Mifflin Company, publishers

For you fare along, on some narrow roadway, through stony labyrinths; huge rock mountains, heaving over your head, on this hand; and under your feet, on that, the roar of winds and echoes howling on you in an almost preternatural manner. Towering rock barriers rise sky high before you, and behind you, and around you. The roadway is narrow, footing none of the best. Sharp turns there are, where it will behoove you to mind your paces; one false step, and you will need no second; in the gloomy jaws of the abyss you vanish, and the spectral winds howl requiem. Somewhat better are the suspension bridges, made of bamboo and leather, though they swing like seesaws; men are stationed with lassos, to gin you dexterously, and fish you up from the torrent, if you trip there.

　　　　　　　—Thomas Carlyle. *Essay on Dr. Francis*

1. So far as you can tell without their context, which, if any, of these three passages come under the derogation of being "fine writing"?

2. What quality preserves from that stigma the one or ones which are not "fine writing"?

3. Choosing what seems to you the worst of the excerpts, analyze its faults.

4. Try improving this same excerpt not by additions but only by elisions. Can it, by cutting only, be made noticeably better?

5. In the second excerpt, the words in the first sentence are forced out of their usual order. Replace them in the usual order. Is the sentence more or less effective?

6. Select three descriptive words (adjectives or adverbs) in each excerpt which seem to you either notably effective or notably ill-chosen.

7. For the ill-chosen descriptive words, supply substitutes.

8. Write a brief description of some scene, natural or man-

made, which shall bring the scene before the reader's eyes and yet be under no suspicion of "fine writing."

B

That night the lobo wolves howled too near, and Mesquite sat up feverishly, reaching for a gun. Turner pushed him back, reassuring, but the wolves worried him too, as they sent their long-drawn, mournful howls back and forth across the small camp. The little pack burros scuttled to the ends of their ropes, and Turner's black stallion gave a shrill trumpet of fear.

Mesquite wanted to get up. "Danged lobos," he muttered, resisting Turner's attempt to quiet him. "Part of this cheatin' desert. It don't want me to have the gold I found."

Turner whipped out his .45 and fired three reverberating shots towards the unseen wolves. One lobo yelped in pain, and the grinding crunch of teeth on bones mingled with loud growling as the pack fell on their wounded member without waiting for death.

It may be that you remember Lashes. He appeared on the outlaw horizon of one of our large cities a few years ago, a unique artist of bank robbery. His career was meteoric in both brilliance and duration. He displayed the practiced hand and composure of an old-timer, yet he was unknown even to other members of his profession. He worked alone, rapidly, skillfully, collected his swag and effected a complete disappearance. After a time the town became too warm, and on several occasions he escaped capture only by the narrowest margin. Finally after he had been trailed to what was alleged to be his hideout, he dropped out of sight and was heard of no more.

1. In the story from which the first of these excerpts is taken, Turner is nursing Mesquite, who has been bitten by a snake. In paragraph four, Turner builds a fire and thus frightens the wolves away. Why does the writer not have him build it sooner?

2. If you were with Turner, what common-sense advice should you give him about his shooting? Why has not the writer applied this common-sense advice for himself?

3. Which of the verbs in the excerpts are effectively used?

4. Is the first excerpt better or worse written than the second?

5. The second excerpt is taken from a detective story. From what point of observation is it written?

6. Given this point of observation, what destructive deviation from it does the writer allow himself?

7. In a detective story, will it be possible to continue with the present point of observation?

8. Contrast the use of verbs in the second excerpt with the use in the first.

9. Limiting yourself to one, what one word or phrase in the second excerpt should you remove? With what should you replace it?

III

(The quotations and questions given in this section are suggestive only. Any reader can readily increase their number for himself.)

1. *The habit of trusting to general assertions and thus sliding away from exact presentation is one no beginner can afford to form.*

a. Give an illustration of an "exact presentation" of character.

b. Change it to generalized statement by removing specific statements.

c. Characterize the same person first by explanation, second by person's action, third by person's speech, fourth by dialogue between two of the person's acquaintances.

2. *No author can compel a reader to carry in mind a dozen differing details.*

a. "Too much of him every way; pervadingly too much nose of a coarse, wrong shape; and his nose in his mind and his manners; too much smile to be real; too much frown to be false; too many large teeth to be visible at once without suggesting a bite." What prevents this characterization from being a presentation by means of many differing details?

b. Write an exact personal description of some individual you know. Underline the phrases, if any, in this exact description which reveal character.

c. For the same person, find a phrase which at once describes and characterizes him.

3. *It is wise for the beginner to make sure that his own mind is clear as to the difference between characterizing a figure and assigning to it certain identifying marks.*

a. Name the "identifying marks" for some stock character in fiction with which you are familiar.

b. What additions and subtractions are needed to change these identifying marks into characterization?

4. *Once the story is under way, character directs circumstance. Happenings must stop dead or change their course if character be altered, for the happenings continue to exist only because of the kind of person on whom they act.*

a. Find, within your family or among your friends, some person whose character does direct circumstance.

b. Set down as briefly as you can what the qualities of spirit are which cause the person to direct circumstance.

c. Are they necessarily amiable or noble qualities?

d. If in your first choice they are, find one in which circumstances are directed by some especial flaw of temper possessed by the person.

e. From your reading, select a person who directs circumstances and note the qualities assigned him by the author which cause him to do so.

5. *Any figure shown in fiction as in control of his own responses to happening is thereby made greater than happening, though not impervious to it.*

a. Turning back to the text, find which of the excerpts given in *Time* may be used to illustrate this quotation.

b. Provide an illustration from your reading.

c. Write a scene in which the person is shown meeting an unfortunate or destructive happening but remaining in control of his own responses to it.

6. *Surprise alone has no fictional value.*

a. Why has it none ?

b. How can fictional value be given it?

c. Does the statement hold true of stories in which the

surprises are in the use of words, not in incident or character—as, for example, in some of O. Henry's stories?

7. *For a beginner, attempts at objective treatment furnish valuable practice, and this whether stories result from the attempts or not.*

    a. Why do they furnish valuable practice?

    b. Select from the text one excerpt told from another point of observation and retell it objectively.

8. *Stream of consciousness is a name well chosen.*

    a. What justification is given for this statement?

    b. Write an account of any three or four minutes of time during a given day as the happenings of those minutes appear in the stream of consciousness of one of the persons concerned.

    c. Rewrite the passage beginning "All the way home it grew worse" (p. 110), giving it objective treatment but not reducing the reader's knowledge of the distress of mind of the main figure.